Carl A. Honeycutt
Reread in Lent 1991

THINGS THAT MATTER

". . . THINGS THAT MATTER —
that will be the title of my next book."

Diary, January 2, 1929

The Presiding Bishop's Book for Lent

THINGS THAT MATTER

The Best of the Writings of

BISHOP BRENT

Edited, with a Biographical Sketch, by

FREDERICK WARD KATES

HARPER & BROTHERS, PUBLISHERS

New York

Acknowledgment is hereby made to Longmans, Green & Co., Inc. and to the Executors of the Estate of the late Bishop Brent for permission to reprint selections from the following books: *Adventure for God, The Consolations of the Cross, Leadership, The Mount of Vision, Presence, Understanding, With God in the World;* to the Diocese of Western New York for the article "Things That Matter"; to Macrae-Smith Company for the selections from *The Conquest of Trouble and the Peace of God* and *With God in Prayer;* to Harper & Brothers for the selections from *Adventures in Prayer,* arranged and edited by S. S. Drury.

F. W. K.

Contents

Foreword

It is a privilege to commend this book to our Church people, clerical and lay, for Lenten reading. This year Bishop Brent has been brought forcibly to our minds and hearts. At the first Assembly of the World Council of Churches his name was mentioned again and again with gratitude to God for his vision and leadership. Also there has just recently been published by the Westminster Press Dean Alexander Zabriskie's splendid life of Bishop Brent. Although he passed from our sight almost twenty years ago, his words are germane to us and to our world. No one can read his article, "Things That Matter," or his reflections upon life and death without an uplift toward God with renewed faith and courage. To those who knew Bishop Brent, these pages will remind us of a revered friend and spiritual guide. For others I believe his message can stand on its own wisdom and power.

Mr. Kates was a member of the Diocese of Western New York. This book is an expression of his indebtedness to Bishop Brent whom he loved and admired. I believe that he and those who have helped make this book possible have wrought well.

HENRY K. SHERRILL
Presiding Bishop

THINGS THAT MATTER

Bishop Brent — *A Biographical Sketch*

The name of Charles Henry Brent flashes instantly upon our attention when we recall the great builders of the reign of God upon earth in modern times. All who knew this rare spirit, refined in the furnace of God, recognized one who had offered up his life on the altar of the service of God in this world. "Courage, wisdom, goodness, and all inspired by grace, were his living sacrifice on the altar of his service of the Church, the one body of Jesus Christ," wrote Principal A. E. Garvie on Good Friday, 1929, upon hearing of his death.

At first a rather shy, diffident clergyman quietly exercising his ministry as an inconspicuous parish priest in a South Boston slum area, Charles Henry Brent developed during the years into one of the most intrepid and gallant ambassadors of Christ the world has known for many years. When he died, the morning of March 27, 1929, in Lausanne, Switzerland, a city which had become a symbol of his life, the Christian world mourned the passing of a tall, somewhat austere, often deeply lonesome, man who had grown during his lifetime into one of contemporary Christendom's foremost leaders, prophets, and seers.

1

A consecrated Christian spirit, a friend of humanity, a servant of God, a gifted writer and commanding preacher, a missionary bishop and statesman, a Christian gentleman, a prophet of world unity, and the twentieth century's greatest champion of and crusader for Christian Unity—Charles Henry Brent has been aptly called "Everybody's Bishop." At home at different times in Canada, Western New York, Massachusetts, the Philippines, the Orient, Europe's battlefields, and England, no corner of the world can claim him as exclusively its own.

A simple grave marker of the recumbent style, designed by Ralph Adams Cram, the Bishop's godson and one of America's leading church architects, and paid for by the contributions of over four thousand people, principally adults and children of his Diocese of Western New York, marks the Bishop's final resting place in the beautiful Bois de Vaux Cemetery, Lausanne. The inscription on this grave marker epitomizes Bishop Brent's life story:

Charles Henry Brent
1862–1929
Bishop of the Philippine Islands
1901–1918
Bishop of Western New York
1918–1929
A Servant of God
A Friend of Humanity
An Apostle of Christian Unity

On one beveled edge are the words:

Chief of Chaplains, American Expeditionary Force—1917–1919

On the other beveled edge is the inscription:

President First World Conference on Faith and Order—1927

These laconic phrases sum up with superb accuracy the life of this splendid Christian spirit of our times. "A servant of God" he certainly was all his life through. To be such, at any rate, was his constant endeavor and his burning desire. In a letter to the secretary of his diocese written from General Headquarters, A.E.F., in France, July 17, 1918, he said: "He [God] knows how honest my purpose is to serve His Kingdom." His deeds and prayers and lifelong efforts demonstrate how truly he was "A Friend of Humanity." As "An Apostle of Christian Unity" he is remembered with veneration by all who are familiar with the history of the Ecumenical Movement and who care for the cause of Christian Reunion with which his name will forever be inseparably associated.

Though born a Canadian, Charles Henry Brent was an American citizen for almost forty years, combining a deep devotion to British ideals and customs with a militant patriotism for the United States. He was born in Newcastle, Canada, a village on Lake Ontario halfway between Toronto and Kingston, on April 9, 1862, the son of the Reverend Canon Henry Brent and his wife Sophia. His father was rector of this rural parish for forty-two years. On his mother's side he was the great-grandson of Thomas Cummings, a New England Loyalist who moved to Canada after the American Revolution. From his earliest memory his mind was set on the ministry. At one time he said, "I do not recall an instant of my life when I aspired to any vocation excepting that of the Ministry, but on one brief occasion when I faced the possibility of becoming a musician. As a boy at school the Ministry seemed to me the one vocation worth considering. Were I again on the threshold of life I would choose as I have chosen."

His education was carried out with a view to his calling. He prepared for college at Trinity College School, Port Hope, Ontario, one of Canada's great boys' schools, and in 1884 he was graduated with classical honors from Trinity College of the University of Toronto. In school and in college he distinguished himself not only as a competent and gifted student but as a formidable athlete. For two years after graduation he acted as undermaster at his preparatory school.

Bishop Sweatman of Toronto ordained Brent to the diaconate in 1886, and the next year elevated him to the priesthood. His first position was curate and organist at St. John's Church, Buffalo, New York, where he remained a year. Then he became curate on the staff of St. Paul's Church (now Cathedral) in Buffalo, in charge of St. Andrew's Mission which at that time was located on Spruce Street. When he attempted to place candles on the altar Bishop Coxe, the diocesan of Western New York, objected. Whereupon he departed for Boston, Massachusetts, where he remained at the Church of St. John the Evangelist from 1888 until 1891, living three and a half years at the Cowley Mission House under the guidance of Fathers Hall, Osborne, and Torbert. There he learned the lessons of an ordered spiritual life—"the indispensable need of securing time for study and devotion and experience in mysticism."

In 1891 Bishop Phillips Brooks placed Father Torbert and Charles Brent in charge of an abandoned church in the south end of Boston which they revived under the name of St. Stephen's Church. Brent was at this time twenty-nine years old. For ten years he remained at St. Stephen's with Father Torbert, the two priests acting together as associate rectors and Brent serving as rector only the last two months.

The years at St. Stephen's were important and valuable ones for the young churchman. His humble work in a struggling parish in a crowded neighborhood of underprivileged people proved good schooling for his naturally aristocratic mind. These years deepened not only his ideas of religion but also his insight into human character. Mingling with the "loafers" on Boston Common helped his heart to grow mellow and his blood to flow warmer. He came to know people, all sorts of people. It was during these "hidden years" that Charles Henry Brent was forged into the man who received, and most worthily, one day in the autumn of 1901 a telegram from San Francisco informing him of his election by the House of Bishops of the Protestant Episcopal Church of the United States as the first Missionary Bishop of the Philippine Islands.

At the time of his election as Bishop of the Philippines, Doctor Rainsford, rector of St. George's, New York City, was considering Brent as "the best man" for the associate with himself in the Manhattan parish.

"He is, of course, a High Churchman," wrote Rainsford to his senior warden, J. Pierpont Morgan, "but he is not as high as when he sought 'the order.' He is a man of God. He is in sympathy with the present time. His eyes are in the front of his head, and not in the back. He can preach. He loves men and understands them. And he is a democrat."

It was in June of the same year, by the way, that his name came up for prominent consideration as Bishop-Coadjutor of Minnesota. Bishop Henry Codman Potter in recommending Doctor Alsop and Charles Henry Brent said of the latter:

"His traditions are those of a modern churchman with sin-

gularly large and noble conceptions of the relation of the
church to humanity. I know no man in the American Church
who is, in some of the highest respects—character, competency
for leadership, enthusiasm, directness, personal attractiveness,
and high spiritual qualities—Mr. Brent's superior."

Such was the man Charles Henry Brent had become by
1901, at thirty-nine years of age, and no further words are
needed to emphasize his caliber and to indicate the high regard in which he was held by high dignitaries and leaders of
the Protestant Episcopal Church at that time.

In the summer of 1902 the young Bishop sailed out to his
island diocese, joining at Suez the Governor-General, William
Howard Taft. It was to a big and pioneer task that he set
forth. The next few years in the Philippines clearly made
manifest to all the ability of the young missionary leader the
Church had sent out to the new island-empire of the United
States.

As a matter of fixed policy, Bishop Brent confined his work
in the Philippines to the army, official government circles, and
the native Moros and Igorots. His was a hard assignment, but
in short order he was winning men to goodness and to Christ
on the basis of their compelling beauty and by the contagion
of his own manly idealism. General John J. Pershing, confirmed by Bishop Brent in Manila in 1910, was but one of a
host of army and government officials who were led into the
Church's fellowship by him.

In the Philippines, Bishop Brent not only gave: he also received. He tells us that "it was among the pagan peoples that
I learned that equality before God of all men, which I count
to be the chief treasure I have honestly made my own in my
lifetime." His experience with the Moros and Igorots was

simply an advanced course in what he had begun to learn in the slum sections of Boston.

The strength of the Protestant Episcopal Church in the Philippines before World War II, during it, and the surety of its revived vigor in the years at hand is testimony to the inspired leadership and energetic labors of Bishop Brent. During his episcopate (1901–1918) hospitals, churches, schools for boys and girls, mission stations, and a great cathedral center were established, the Bishop always building boldly for a large future.

It was while resident in the Orient, on the frontier of Christianity, that the desperate need for a united Christendom impinged forcibly on Bishop Brent's still forming mind. Here it was that he pledged himself to labor for the cause of Christian Reunion all his days.

His Philippine Islands ministry was frequently interrupted by trips back to the United States. Bishop Brent always enjoyed the rest and leisure of these long sea voyages which gave him opportunity for reading, meditation, and writing.

The young missionary leader was sought as their leader by many dioceses during these years. In 1908 he declined a call to become Bishop of Washington, D.C. Two times more he was called and two times more he refused. He was also elected to and declined the bishopric of New Jersey.

It was during the first decade of the new century that Bishop Brent rose into national and international prominence. The priest, who not so many years before had seriously considered entering the monastic life, was at this time equally at home in the hut of a Moro savage or a diplomatic embassy. And it was during this period that we witness Bishop Brent more than winning his spurs as a diplomat and statesman.

The greatest evil in Filipino society, Bishop Brent and the government soon discovered, was opium, and to its extirpation Bishop Brent directly bent his efforts. Within a year after the official party of the island governor-general had assumed their duties, a commission had been appointed to investigate the use of and traffic in opium and the laws regarding such use and traffic in Japan, Formosa, Shanghai, Hong Kong, Saigon, Singapore, Burma, Java, and the Philippine Islands. Major E. C. Carter, U.S. Army, Dr. José Albert and Bishop Brent comprised the commission. The commission assembled August 13, 1903, at Manila and gathered data until February 5, 1904. Then from February 8, 1904, until March 15, 1904, the committee sat daily and finally presented its report. Briefly, the plan recommended was for opium to become a government monopoly immediately, this to become prohibition, except for medical purposes, after three years.

But the work of this opium commission was but introductory to the great International Opium Conference at Shanghai during February, 1909, over which Bishop Brent sat as president, which was dominated by his leadership and vision, and which was by him single-handedly brought to a happy outcome. Bishop Brent also acted as chief commissioner of the American delegation to this meeting. He again served as chairman of a United States delegation to an international opium conference in 1911 and 1912 at The Hague.

By the outbreak of World War I, Bishop Brent was a world-renowned figure, a friend of national leaders in many countries, a citizen of the world, a foremost leader in the affairs of his Church. Though he was an ardent lover of peace, he accepted as a high privilege and as his duty the invitation of

General Pershing, a friend of old standing, to act as Senior Headquarters Chaplain of the American Expeditionary Force.

Bishop Brent's war career is really a separate story by itself. He stands with the late G. A. Studdert-Kennedy, "Dick" Sheppard and Cardinal Mercier as one of the men whose contribution to the moral and spiritual tone of the Allied fighting forces was a real help in winning the war. To the Bishop, the war was an unmitigated disaster and tragedy. He entertained great hopes that out of it great things for the welfare of the nations would issue.

Popularly known as "the khaki-colored bishop," Bishop Brent was all through the dark days of war a pillar of idealism and a tower of moral strength. He was frequently employed as a good-will ambassador smoothing out friction between organizations engaged in war work or on a high diplomatic errand ironing out friction between nations. He was a constant and constructive interpreter between the United States and Great Britain, and it was entirely natural and fitting that General Pershing should choose him to deliver his message in 1918 to the men of the British and American fleets in the North Sea. He used all the prestige of his position to secure action from the French government in suppressing the organized vice which threatened the morality of the army. And the present structure of the Army Chaplains' Corps owes much to his recommendations based on his experience as the Chief-of-Chaplains in World War I.

The war years were for Bishop Brent a soul-searching experience. If into the war Bishop Brent went a priest, he came out of it a prophet. Deeply baptized in suffering, shocked by the brutality and carnage of warfare, more international than ever before in his outlook and influence, he now added one more cause to those which he served—the cause of permanent peace. He struggled for it all the rest of his life.

The war ended a chapter in Bishop Brent's life, as it did for many another man. He did not return to his missionary bishopric in the Orient, but went to Western New York. He had been elected bishop of the diocese in October, 1917, and assumed jurisdiction in January, 1918, though at the time he was overseas with the American troops in France. The diocese had a bishop and a great bishop—yet it had him not, and it was not to have him actually in residence and at his task until May, 1919.

Bishop Brent's coming into the Diocese of Western New York, according to the secretary of the diocese at the time, the Rev. G. Sherman Burrows, "was like a strong fresh breeze stirring up heavy atmosphere." In no time at all Bishop Brent had measured his task and had it in hand. He gave of his best to his diocese, faithfully fulfilling his episcopal duties, discharging the myriad tasks that fell to his hand, and firing the churchmen of the diocese with his own vision. He made his home in the See House, Buffalo, and took care of the western half of the diocese while Bishop Ferris, his suffragan, lived in Rochester and took charge of the eastern half (since 1931 the Diocese of Rochester).

In one sense the diocese paid a penalty for having so eminent a leader for its head: the Bishop was continually called away from the diocese on some high errand or important mission; but the diocese was proud to have its bishop a man of such stature and one devoting himself to the causes to which he pledged his energies during the ten years of his actual administration of the diocese which proved to be the climaxing and last years of his life. The Bishop was engaged in big matters, befitting a big man; and in his greatness he swept the diocese along with him. It was not possible to think and plan and function along narrow lines or on petty, provincial levels with him as leader or, in his own words, "foremost companion."

Accomplishments in diocesan administration during Bishop Brent's episcopate included naming a suffragan bishop in 1920; organizing an executive council for the diocese with special departments for missions, religious education, etc.; establishing of associate missions in rural counties; greater giving especially for missions; improved religious education and strengthening of diocesan lay organizations. The diocese, during the years of Bishop Brent's episcopate, rose as never before to a sense of mission extending far beyond its borders. It was rudely shaken into something of this larger vision by the part America played in World War I. It more definitely took steps to live up to that vision when it gave the Bishop to the A.E.F. as Senior Chaplain. And it was influenced even more in the direction of the wider interests when the Bishop took up his life in the diocese. His mind, heart, effort, and vision embraced all mankind. Diocesan and national boundaries were simply landmarks, not mind limits or heart limits. He knew no geographic borders restricting the duty Christians owe all mankind. Thus the diocese, under Bishop Brent's leadership and the magnificent inspiration he gave it, was happy and proud to make its contribution to the world's need. If Bishop Brent went abroad on some Christian mission, Western New York churchmen felt the diocese went abroad with him. If the Bishop accomplished something good for the great body of humanity, the diocese felt it was having its hand in his accomplishments by supporting and abetting him. Under these circumstances Bishop Brent felt little to restrain him in his journeyings and undertakings.

Among the many calls that came to him during the years of residence in Buffalo, New York, were serving as Chancellor of Hobart College, Geneva, New York, one of the Episcopal Church colleges in the United States; serving as a member of the Board of Overseers of Harvard University; in the spring of 1921 delivering the Duff Lectures at the Universities of Edinburgh, Aberdeen, and Glasgow; in the summer of 1923, on President Harding's appointment, acting on the Advisory Committee on Narcotics of the League of Nations in Geneva, Switzerland; in 1924 attending the International Opium Conference at Geneva, Switzerland; in 1925 opening the public sessions of the Conference on Life and Work at Stockholm making an address on "International Relations"; during 1926 to 1928 functioning as Bishop-in-charge of the American Episcopal Churches in Europe; and, finally, presiding over the First World Conference on Faith and Order in Lausanne in 1927.

"We have only just begun to realize how much of the prewar period is done with for good and for all, and how much that is new is beginning," said the late Bishop Charles Henry Brent in a posthumous volume, *The Commonwealth*, published in 1930.

Fully aware of "how much that is new is beginning," Bishop Brent set out after World War I to be a prophet of the new era, and increasingly during his latter years we find him speaking forth, not only as a world citizen and as a great churchman and Christian statesman, but as a clarion-voiced, clear-eyed, confident prophet of things to come.

The burden of his message and its constant refrain was unity and peace. Repeatedly he preached on these subjects and more and more his public utterances became less sermons and more prophecies and fragments of visions.

The realm of God on earth, the commonwealth, he viewed as all peoples living together in harmony and in peace, united one to another and each and all to God, the common Father, in the Church of Christ. The alternatives before the world, he felt, were "unity or confusion, peace or war." So he bent his every effort toward the progress of the causes of permanent world peace and organic Christian Unity.

"It is our creative responsibility to shape the world and make it according to a pattern given to us by God," he declared. And this pattern is that of a world at peace, for "war, or organized destruction, is the negation of society; unity, or organized construction, is fulfillment."

"I have seen too much [of war] and know too much," remarked Premier Clemenceau of France after World War I. "If I wrote my memoirs, not a man would go to war, even if the security of his country demanded it." The spiritual revulsion from war Clemenceau experienced was in an even more heightened degree the reaction of Bishop Brent. He emerged from his war duty as Chief-of-Chaplains, A.E.F., permanently burdened by war's suffering and with his heart chilled by the horror, tragedy, and grim futility of warfare.

Before the war Bishop Brent was a staunch and almost militantly patriotic American, in a tempered though robust Theodore Rooseveltian manner, but we find this entry in his diary, dated January 28, 1918, which reflects a changed attitude:

"The horrors of war and its savagery increase. God grant

that we may in the end declare to all ages the futility of force as an agent of God's Kingdom."

Although the League of Nations was only a partial fulfillment of his ideal, he hailed it with hearty approval as a step in the right direction, and it was with particular fitness that he was the person chosen to open its first assembly with prayer.

The older he grew the more the Bishop felt it was the solemn duty of the Christian Church to remove from war the spiritual sanction which for centuries it had been accorded and to do all in its power to make war repugnant to the consciences of Christian people.

At the 1925 Stockholm Conference on Christian Life and Work he said: "It is for the Church to determine in which circumstances, if any, killing and maiming, lying and guile, destruction and rapine, in short, the declaration of a moratorium of the moral law, ceases to be an offense against God and man and becomes a praiseworthy virtue and patriotic duty. Dare we do less than hold that war as an institution for the settlement of international disputes by brute force and allied to skill in cunning and lying, is incompatible with the mind of Christ, and therefore incompatible with the mind of His Church?"

The Bishop's last great sermon, delivered in Canterbury Cathedral, November 25, 1928, four months before his death, is filled with the luster of his glorious idealism. It was both as a statesman of the world and as a Christian mystic that he spoke and made his last confession:

"I am not ashamed to bare my soul to you. I glory in the fact that an incomparable vision holds me in its gracious thrall. It is not so much that I possess it as that it possesses me. My vision is of a world in the here and now at peace and unity with itself."

In one of his greatest sermons, "Prisoners of Hope," preached in the Cathedral at Manila, September 20, 1914, Bishop Brent described the peace he believed it was God's intention the world should have. It is a peace that money cannot buy, nor wisdom concoct, nor force capture. It will come only as a result of supremest effort. It is a peace that will not come by wishful thinking or just hoping. It is no passionless peace, mere quiescence, but rather a peace that is the highest and most creative form of energy.

"I am not an advocate of peace that has as its goal and motive ease and the love of ease," he declared in another sermon. "Peace, if I understand its meaning, has no room in its mansions for the idle or the cowardly. The demands of peace are more exacting than those of war. When we pass from war to peace we pass from compulsory to volitional effort, from necessity to choice. Because we forget this, peace falls into disrepute. The forces of evil are organized and active frequently when those of righteousness are lolling in slippered ease."

"We are prisoners of hope," said Bishop Brent in the Manila sermon mentioned above. "We believe in an ultimate permanent peace. . . . We believe peace is God's settled order, peace, social, industrial, international, and that it will be the distinguishing note of human life as soon as men are willing."

The necessity for a reunited Church was the strongest claim laid upon Bishop Brent during the years that followed World War I and until his death in 1929. As far back as 1907, when he came from the Oriental missionary frontier of the Philippine Islands to the United States to attend the General Convention of the Protestant Episcopal Church, he felt with an almost consuming passion the poignant and desperate need for a reunited Christian Church. "The unity of Christendom is not a luxury," he said at that time, electrifying the Convention. "The world will go limping until Christ's prayer that all may be one is answered."

From every angle he saw the imperative need for an organically reunited Christendom. Divided Christendom had failed, though, indeed, God had used it far "beyond anything we had a right to expect." Bishop Brent felt organic unity was necessary for survival alone, as well as to overcome the stigma and scandal and blasphemy of division. For efficiency and that the Church might have a sharp cutting edge in dealing with practical moral, social, economic, and political matters, Bishop Brent championed the cause with which his name is indelibly identified. As a Christian statesman, he realized that until the Church could give its united witness upon such matters as sex relations, marriage, divorce, the use of force, class hatreds, racial antagonisms, social injustice, education, and international problems, the greatest force for righteousness would be lacking in modern life.

The scandal of a divided Church impelled Bishop Brent to fight for unity. "Disorder in the Church, the Body of Christ, is sacrilege and blasphemy," he said. The divisions in Christendom, he believed, "present a moral affront to the enterprise inaugurated by Jesus Christ and constitute the outstanding limitation of its progress. They are an essential denial of His Spirit of love and fellowship and a misuse of the resources of His followers."

Bishop Brent learned from his own experience in the Philippines that a splintered Church cannot succeed in its task of conversion. "Do not be deceived," he admonished; "without unity the conversion of great nations is well-nigh hopeless."

Passing over in this place further discussion of Bishop Brent's reasons for pressing the cause of Christian Reunion, his appraisal of the obstacles to unity, and his thoughts on how to achieve unity, all of which are presented in Chapter 2 of this book in his own words, it is important to note here that he came to believe increasingly in the merits of what has come to be known as the "Faith and Order" method. Specifically, this approach is the encouragement of the coming together of Christians of different traditions with the single purpose of seeking to grow in mutual understanding of one another's beliefs and practices, resolutely putting aside any desire to convert one another or to prove the superiority or deficiency o- this or that type of Christian faith and order, seeking conf stantly to clear away misconceptions, and to win knowledge and appreciation of that which calls forth the loyalty of others.

The crowning event of Bishop Brent's life was, without any doubt, the First World Conference on Faith and Order which convened in Lausanne, Switzerland, on August 3, 1927, and which sat in session until August 21. Bishop Brent preached on "The Call to Unity" at the opening service. "The call to unity is primarily from God to man," he declared. "It is for our own good that the appeal is made. Through unity alone can the Kingdom of God be set up among men. Through unity alone can the world believe and know that the Father has sent Jesus Christ to reveal Him to the whole human race. It stands as the unalterable condition on which He can fulfill His mission to mankind. This no one doubts who accepts Jesus Christ as Lord and Saviour."

As president of the conference, Bishop Brent won not only the approval but the admiration and affection of the 400 delegates who had assembled from 40 different nations and represented 108 autonomous, non-Romanist Christian communions. This memorable conclave of churchmen in a very real sense was due to Bishop Brent's vision and persevering labors over seventeen years. "All the prayers and desires and labors of seventeen years meet in this hour," were his words in his conference-opening address. In his diary under date of October 5, 1910, is this entry: "At the morning Eucharist there came vividly before me the possibility of a World Conference on Faith and Order." It might accurately be said that the Lausanne Conference of 1927 was born during the sessions of the World Missionary Conference at Edinburgh in 1910, though the actual initiation of the movement took place at the General Convention of the Protestant Episcopal Church of the United States meeting in October of 1910 at Cincinnati, Ohio. Bishop Brent had returned from the Edinburgh Conference feeling that the scope of that meeting was too strictly limited— it concerned itself only with practical questions of missionary statesmanship and policy. He went before the General Convention at Cincinnati, asking whether leaders of the churches, responsibly appointed, might not meet for the patient discussion of those matters of Faith (doctrine and belief) and Order (polity and government) which had been so rigorously excluded from the agenda of the recent Edinburgh Conference. The result was the adoption by the Convention of a resolution authorizing the appointment of a joint commission of seven bishops, seven presbyters, and seven laymen "to bring about a

Conference for the consideration of questions touching Faith and Order, and that all Christian communions throughout the world which confess our Lord Jesus Christ as God and Saviour be asked to unite with us in arranging for and conducting such a Conference."

Thus the Faith and Order Movement was born. The fruition of Bishop Brent's labors was in large measure achieved in August, 1948, when the World Council of Churches was organized in Amsterdam.

His work for Church Unity through the Faith and Order Movement was Bishop Brent's major interest after World War I and until his death. It possessed him and permeated him. It seemed to some that his zeal for unity was leading him to minimize certain fundamentals of Christian doctrine. He was criticized particularly for the breadth of his definition of the Catholic Church and especially for his latitudinarianism with regard to Holy Orders.

Bishop Brent was in England during the fall of 1928 in order to attend the enthronement of the new Archbishop of Canterbury as the representative of the Protestant Episcopal Church. After this high occasion, he did not return to America, as he had planned, but remained in England, acting upon the advice of his physician, Sir Thomas Barlow. During these weeks he was the guest of the American Ambassador to the Court of St. James, the Hon. Alanson B. Houghton, and he spent his days in quiet and comfort, seeking renewal of his strength. Each morning he either conducted or participated in a brief service in the Embassy and during these days he saw much of Lord Davidson, the retired Archbishop of Canterbury, an old friend of many years' standing.

Apparently somewhat improved in health, and with the hope of gaining still more vigor, he undertook, in March, 1929, a trip across the continent, through Switzerland to the Mediterranean, where he and Sir Thomas were to embark on the yacht "Asia" for a leisurely cruise. He arrived in Paris on Thursday evening, March 21. The next day he visited with the Very Rev. Frederick W. Beekman, D.D., Dean of the American Pro-Cathedral Church of the Holy Trinity in Paris, and also had a long talk with his wartime chief, General Pershing. He stayed in Paris over Sunday, which was Palm Sunday, attending the late service. The Dean of the General Theological Seminary, New York, the Very Rev. Hughell E. W. Fosbroke, D.D., was the preacher. The next morning he departed for Switzerland, stopping at Lausanne to break the journey. It was here in the city which has become the enduring symbol of his life and of his greatest contribution to Christendom that Bishop Brent died on March 27, 1929, as he read from his Book of Common Prayer "A Commendatory Prayer for a Sick Person at the point of Departure."

The burial service was conducted in Christ Church (Anglican), Lausanne, on Friday, April 12, by Dean Beekman in the presence of a notable company of distinguished persons, including Ambassador Houghton. The musical portions of the service were rendered by the choir of the Russian Church (Greek Orthodox) of Geneva, while the prayers recited in English, French, and German by assisting German and French pastors testified to the hold the late leader exercised over peoples of many nations. At the cemetery the Mayor of Lausanne spoke and the Rev. Dr. Adolph Keller pronounced the Benediction.

Twelve days later, April 24, St. Paul's Cathedral, Buffalo,

was thronged by a vast congregation attending a memorial service for the Bishop. The preacher was the Rt. Rev. Arthur C. A. Hall, D.D., Bishop of Vermont, a lifelong friend from Cowley days in Boston. Bishop Hall had preached at Bishop Brent's Consecration in Emmanuel Church, Boston, on December 19, 1901, and also at the Farewell Service in Calvary Church, New York City, six months later on the eve of Brent's departure for the Philippines. The late Bishop of Washington, the Rt. Rev. James E. Freeman, D.D., preached at a similar service held in Christ Church, Rochester, on May 10.

Bishop Brent, in his lifetime, was honored by many academic bodies and the governments of several nations. He held three degrees from Trinity College, Toronto, and honorary degrees awarded him by King's College, Harvard University, Yale University, University of Glasgow, Columbia University, the University of Rochester, Union College, the University of Toronto, and New York University. With humble pride he wore the Distinguished Service Medal of the United States and the ribbons of a Commander of the Order of Leopold of Belgium, Companion of the Bath of Great Britain, and Officer of the Legion of Honor of France.

The death of Bishop Brent brought keen sorrow to the hearts of all who knew and loved him, and to all who cared for the great cause of Christian Reunion to the service of which he had given his uttermost farthing of strength and had devoted his every talent and gift. He had literally burned out his life in service of the overmastering ideal to which he had pledged his life. Lausanne, the scene of the inspiring conference of 1927, is properly his resting place.

As Bishop in a great communion of the Church of God, and, in the opinion of many, its noblest son; as a faithful and consecrated servant of God; as a friend of all humanity; as an apostle of Christian Unity; as a prophet of a world dwelling in harmony and in peace; as a spiritual leader of fighting men in wartime; as a gifted preacher, brilliant lecturer, and able writer; as one who was truly a man of God; and as President of the First World Conference on Faith and Order, Charles Henry Brent, "one of God's noblemen," will long be held in honor. Surely it may be said of him what he himself said at the grave of Willard Straight at Suresne Cemetery during the war: "Death cannot conquer so knightly a soul."

"There are two types of successful men," Bishop Charles Lewis Slattery once wrote. "One type undertakes only such tasks as can be completed triumphantly within a definite time. These men announce their reasonable goal, and then, in their own lifetime, attain it. Brent was of the higher type, which dared to gaze far beyond the limits of one man's life, or of the immediate century or age. An adventurer he was on uncharted seas."

Said Principal Garvie, his deputy at Lausanne, on learning of his death: "That he is with us no longer to lead, is a call to us all to follow more closely his invisible leader."

· *1* ·

Things That Matter[1]

In my absence you, my dear people, still abide in my heart and memory. It is about as painful a discipline as I could undergo to keep away from work, especially after having made such explicit plans as I published to you in the fall.

At the time I left America, ostensibly on an official errand, really of necessity, I demurred a little and felt some conscience about leaving. Now, however, I recognize how wise it was. When I return to you in the spring I shall hope to have, at any rate, much more vigor than at any time within the past two years.

There are various things that I wish to lay before you, both pastors and people. None of them is new to my mind. All have come vividly and constantly before me, especially in the quiet of the past year when my chief activity has been thought. There are innumerable things of which I could speak but I must confine myself to that which is indispensable and basic.

[1] This article, the last from his pen, was completed by Bishop Brent on February 4, 1929, while he was a guest at the American Embassy in London. It was addressed to the clergy and laity of his diocese and was published in *Our Diocesan Fellowship*, Vol. 9, Nos. 3, 4, and 5, March, April and May, 1929.

I remember how, shortly after my College days, the Professor of Classics lay dying. He was a man of extraordinary gifts, a graduate of Oxford, who imparted to me that love of the classics which has formed the basis of such education as I have. A mutual friend was visiting him and discussing the new commentaries on the Bible. After listening with interest Professor Boys said: "Mr. C.— The best commentary of the Bible is the edge of the grave." I now know what he meant. At the moment I may have thought it was a morbid thought. My experience of the past twelve months and more has shown me that the Valley of the Shadow of Death is a highly illumined valley and is more akin to a mountain top which reveals long views and endless vistas, than it is to a place of gloom. It is not with any sense of fear, but with an extraordinary clearness in one's estimate of values that one views the world from the edge of the grave. During the period of my enforced idleness I have been trying to estimate persons and things from what seemed to me my extraordinary vantage ground on the borders of the world of eternity.

First of all, I would say that it has given me a new zest of life as we know it, and a yearning desire to live longer in this world which is so full of extraordinary wealth in thought and idealism, so abundant in its opportunities for adventure, and so full of God and His purpose. So what I say will not be in any sense valetudinarian but rather, as I hope, as youth might view it, and with an unbounded expectation for the coming generation and those who share with it its best aspirations and hopes.

Standing supreme above all else is God, and what comes from God, which constitute the only Reality. This being so man's chief vocation is to penetrate through the things of sight and sense, and to establish and consummate relationship of a personal character with God. There is nothing that can take the place of this, and without it life loses such effectiveness as it might otherwise have. As the background of all other activities the chief aim of life should be to bring the "Unchanging into the changeable." In these days which are so full of activity and the desire for self-expression, there would seem to be little time for that habit of contemplation which is essential for this preliminary task. All one can say is, that activity without the background of relationship with God is apt to be footless, even mischievous, and "without God in the world." Again, without it, self can never have anything real to express. So-called self-expression becomes mere froth. By contemplation I do not mean musing over things with a desire to put them immediately into some concrete form, but rather the establishment of that friendship toward God which God has toward men. This for its own sake. This is the gem in the casket. The monastic life was an extreme endeavor to embody this truth in practice. Somewhere in Westcott's works he refers to the passage in Plato where the gods, at fixed periods, contemplate the mysteries of absolute truth in order to renew their being. I am not suggesting something that is for gods or for the picked few only. It is an activity of the soul open to all, more especially for those who, like myself, are blessed by special privilege. I recall how Stonewall Jackson is reported to have retired into himself every day to devote his powers, for a considerable period, to the consideration of abstract truths. He had nothing to aid him excepting a blank wall and his mind. How little we are accustomed to this practice we can realize when we consider what a long period two or three minutes of unbroken silence for an intensive effort seems to us. A proper use of it, so far from detracting from man's practical capacity, adds to it enormously. It gives him a background of concentration, spirituality and conviction, as well as that unconsciousness of self which is the secret of all true service. A background of God-consciousness should form the canvas upon which all life is painted. It should stand as the accompaniment to the song, as the sky to the moon and stars, as the verdure to the landscape.

Few persons can conscientiously say they have no time for it. It is a matter of will. Fifteen minutes a day of intensive effort Godward can change the whole complexion of life, raising it from weakness to power, from bondage to liberty.

The inner forces of personality reach their zenith in the exercise of faith. The key to the Christian life is that we walk by faith and not by sight. This was formulated by Habakkuk and reiterated by St. Paul whose main theme it is.[2] Faith does not run counter to reason. It transcends reason and might be legitimately called superknowledge, just as reason is the superfaculty of animal instinct. There is a place where reason ends and faith goes on with steady tread. The higher mystics reach a stage when, instead of saying "I believe" they say, as St. John does in his Epistles, "I know."[3]

No great occupation can be pursued without faith, faith which operates irrespective of its object. Science, for instance, is as dependent upon it as religion. This very day I read an article by Eddington in which he tells how the atom of negative electricity, commonly known as the electron, is a hypothesis and "a dummy." To postulate its existence faith as much as reason is required. This may seem a little bit abstruse but in

[2] Hab. 2:4; Gal. 3:11.
[3] I John 2:3; 5:18, 19, 20.

practice it immediately takes an easily intelligible shape, viz.: in prayer, although I would say that prayer is not the only religious expression, though it is an outstanding articulation of faith. The personality in ourselves approaches the personality of God and life mingles with Life. Faith is a habit rather than an act. Prayer spoken and written is the most refined and beautiful representative act by which we can become capable of keeping up and developing that contact with God which thus derives from Him, in growing volume, the knowledge of Him in which stands our eternal life. To express what we know is one of the most effective ways of learning more. There are some people who say that they cannot pray without a book. Would it not be truer to say, without a pen, they cannot pray coherently? The pen is an aid to express in explicit terms what the mind, without such stimulus, may be incapable of doing. One reason why the liturgical gift of writing collects seems to have died out is because individuals have ceased to write for themselves their aspirations Godward which, in the early days, bore fruit in immortal Collects. You cannot write, with the same power, for others as you write for God and your own edification. "To the glory of God" has a superb meaning, intelligible only to those whose life is "Hid with Christ in God."

I do not wish to make prayer seem abstruse but practical. It may be, it is, hard to pray well, but it is harder for a complex, un-unified life, to pray than for a simple and unlearned. It is more within the reach of a child than a savant. But it is as available as it is indispensable for every one. Put into sincere prayer the amount of effort you do into a game or into your business and you will prevail. To me prayer is the key that unlocks heaven and opens the door to the deep understanding of human life.

Our use of the unseen stretches of life determines what we think, say and do in society. Given a right and industrious use of our conscious moments on the secret side of the veil, and all will be in the burning noonday of active life. In these golden moments, contemplation and prayer, pertinacious and as unbroken as the links of an endless chain, stand in regal dignity governing the whole sweep of life.

What I have thus far said must sound, apart from all other considerations, cold, uninviting and metallic. Standing alone it is an appeal without a motive. Stern theology, or theology divorced from human experience, is of no account and can never win more than lip loyalty. In what I have already said, taken by itself, there is not even a moral appeal. Yet it stands as the premise for all that wealth of Christian thought and life which is the joy and hope of mankind. I admit, however, that the thought of fellowship with God, personal and intimate, which is peculiar to Christianity, is not wholly barren of winsomeness. It stands as the touchstone of all true religion.

The fire that sets the furnace burning, the light that illumines the whole vast realm of existence, comes through the one radiating fact of history. This fact is a Figure with arms stretched out, to the right hand and to the left, backward and forward, touching all the past and all the future. Jesus Christ is not a theory or an idea, but key-personality. He takes His place in our human nature and has His home in a given spot, at a fixed moment of time, like all of us. Let me say at once, without argument, that I accept Him as the highest possible expression of God in human life that man is capable of comprehending and receiving. In that man is made in God's image—a postulate I do not stop to vindicate—it is the human in God which constitutes the connecting link with man. Unless God has entered into human life and justified the assertion that He may be known by man, nothing remains for us but the dreary blankness of agnosticism. The coming in the flesh of Jesus Christ was the manifestation of what God's character always was rather than the taking on of a new character. To quote words which are incomparable— "The Word was made flesh, and dwelt among us (and we beheld His glory, the glory of the only begotten of the Father), full of grace and truth." (I do not think that "the Word" has any Alexandrian connotations. It simply means the expression of the mind of God in terms understandable to the common people—God's self-shewing.) It is the human in God which makes the connecting link with man. Those of the human race who came before Him looked forward toward His coming, those who were born after look back at the historic fact which justified the hope of the earlier generation. All, past and present, look up at the unchangeable God. Man in God is God in man.

This I believe to be the pivotal truth of all truths. There may be, and are, a variety of deductions drawn from the fact, and controversy may rage around the means used for embracing the fact, but it is the fact that counts and not the theories about it. It is the Incarnation and not what we think about it that is the great operating force in the world today, and it will continue to be throughout the ages. The coming of Jesus Christ into the world was and is the outward symbol and most notable illustration of the impetuous, irresistible rush of God manward which has never ceased for the tiniest fragment of time since time was.

Now what does all this mean except that God reveals Himself in the face of a hostile nature "red with raven, tooth and claw," as Love? Little child and learned adult, lowly and high, dolt and savant, alike respond to hot, pulsating love. Nothing else can reach every one. Love is ambitious in its passion to win the last and the least, the vagrant outcast and the wandering lamb. "Love is life and life is love."

> There is no good of life but love—but love!
>   What else looks good, is some shade flung from love;
> Love gilds it, gives it worth. Be warned by me,
>   Never cheat yourself one instant! Love,
> Give love, ask only love, and leave the rest!

Is it necessary to attempt to define love? It is undefinable for "God is Love" and no human language can explain God or do more than faintly picture Him.

It is not my idea, or any human idea, of love which I wish to present. It is love as Jesus Christ revealed it by living it, for Christ came to show us what God, that is Love, is like. To have an inadequate idea of Christ is to have an imperfect understanding of love, for Christ is Love. The knowledge of the New Testament and especially of that section of it which portrays Christ is very incomplete in most of us. We snatch at paragraphs and texts that appeal to us and let go by unheeded the balance. But we have to take the bitter with the sweet, the sternness with the gentleness, the incomprehensible with the easily understood, the uncompromising hates as well as the loves of Christ, if we are to get a proper conception of Him as representing the God of Love. Would it not be a salutary exercise to read through the entire group of Gospels keeping in mind the one thought of love in order at the close of our study to sum up the meaning of love as lived by Christ? Of course mere head knowledge gets us nowhere. Everything that we read must be turned into a personal relationship with the living Christ if it is to become a glowing influence in our lives. To know love is to test it and we come to know it in the testing.

There are a few things which we can say concerning love, generalizing from a survey of the Gospels.

1. Love hates evil with a hate that consumes. Christ's hostility to evil as the enemy of His beloved is the hostility of a flaming white light. The origin of evil He does not reveal, and all our best speculations relative to its origin are futile. He makes it vivid by giving it personality, as, for instance, in the typical temptations. I am not attempting to interpret these personalizations but simply mentioning the fact. Further He takes evil as it is and makes it the foil of His magnificent victories. He expects us to achieve like victories—He in us and we in Him. If He achieves a conquest, it is with the postulate of temptation lying behind it. If He rises from the dead, it is with the grave as a background. I know of no more striking phrase in all Christian literature than the words of St. Paul, "He became sin for us."

There are those who say that love can never give pain. I do not believe it for one minute, nor will the Scriptures concerning Christ sustain such a theory. How about those terrific woes which He pronounced against the Scribes and Pharisees? How about that searching passage at the end of the 25th chapter of St. Matthew where He speaks of His rejection of those who fail in the cardinal works of mercy? But this I would say, that where He does give pain it is always salutary pain, never pain for vengeance' sake but always for a remedial purpose. It is this that makes us eagerly reach up in pain to identify our will with His. In it is the victory that overcometh the world.[4]

[4] I John 5:4.

2. Love exalts righteousness with a zeal that inspires. Today mere moralists are floundering. They are looking for new foundations on which to build a moral system and are having great difficulty to discover them. Righteousness, apart from the righteousness of Christ, has no firm standing ground. Any readjustment of morals must come back to the clear teaching of Christ which is based on the Ten Commandments but which far transcends them by its positive precepts. The Ten Commandments are as the dawn, whereas the righteousness of Christ, simpler far than they, is as high noontide. I do not hesitate to say that Christianity is the only religion, saving Judaism, in all the realm of history that has given a high morality based solely on the mind of God and attainable through a personal interflow of His life and ours through the operation of His Spirit.

3. "Perfect love casteth out fear." Here is a test of the reality of our Christian belief. There is no enemy so absolutely deadly as fear in all of its ghastly aspects—worry, anxiety, panic through the whole gamut of its terrors. A surrendered life, living day by day in the atmosphere of God's love and walking by faith is forever emancipated from fear. Of course I do not mean emancipation from that awe or wonder with which we look at the great unknown stretches of God's majesty. That kind of fear is the beginning of wisdom.

In our materialistic age we are apt to attach too much importance to the gifts of comfort and competence for which most men strain themselves, but the life of prayer, if it is genuine and true, keeps the soul day by day in the clear sunlight of God's protecting love. Probably the greatest fear that most people have is of that plunge into the unknown (or dimly known) which comes through death. Shakespeare has never impressed me as being a devout man but he had a fine type of religion which crops out again and again in his dramas. Here for instance is what he says about the fear of death:

> Cowards die many times before their deaths;
> The valiant never taste of death but once;
> Of all the wonders that I yet have heard,
> It seems to me most strange that men should fear;
> Seeing that death, the necessary end,
> Will come when it will come.

There come to my mind those amazing words of St. Paul where he says, "Jesus Christ has abolished death and brought to light life and incorruption."

There are many other striking features of the love of God as revealed in Christ, but I must leave you to search these out in your study of the Scriptures. I shall confine myself now more to the simpler elements of love which are irresistible in their attractive power and which no one would care to dispute. If we walk by faith we walk in love—both of these phrases are Scriptural and complementary.[5] If we accept faith as our rule of life, we make love a landscape in which we put faith into active practice.

I would not be so foolish as to suppose that love can be so adequately described in words as to kindle love for God through Christ in the hearts of men. Let it suffice only that our love be God high and man wide. I suppose a few have been converted to the love of God or of man by an article in a newspaper, a book, or even a sermon. Books are for edification, but conversion can come only through personal contacts. The Bible alone stands out as the one book capable of all things, so that when I speak of the love of God, it is with no ulterior motive,

[5] Gal. 3:11; 2 John v. 6.

but simply to bear my own witness to its height and depth, its breadth and length. Most people who do not learn it as little children are startled into it through its healing power in sickness, in rescue from some crisis or, most frequently, in the compassionate and complete forgiveness of sins which relieves of the burden and washes the stain, leaving the soul face to face with infinite Love. Love is most often born of gratitude for startling mercies. Nor can it ever begin with us. The torch of God's love must light our little lamp.

Faith and love then are the only bonds of union, unless perhaps we include hope which always seems to me part of faith, uniting us to God. They mingle and interflow. I can never put means of an external character on the same plane as these eternal qualities. We are slow to recognize that there are two fundamental differences in the constitution of mankind. It is not a matter of training but rather of disposition and temperament. There are those who place the accent upon external authority, organization and sacrament, and again there are those who place the accent on the direct ascent of the soul to God. There may be, and is, movement from each group to the other but the two clear distinctions have ever lived and will ever live. The Church into which I was born has a comprehensive character. Unfortunately there are those who injure this character by assuming that the position which they hold is exclusive and who spend their time in controversy with those who hold the other position, and strive to win them. The result is that each helps the other to consolidate his position. Perhaps at one time I indulged in this folly; now, while I recognize the value to me and to many of the sacramental approach which nothing can ever impair so far as I am concerned, I also recognize that there are those to whom all the world is a sacrament and who depend chiefly, sometimes wholly, on the inner approach and the mystical element in religion; whether or no we stress the sacramental, this inner element is indispensable.

My lesser loyalty is to the communion of which I am a member. I can see nothing but disaster in matching religions. It is not the Christian game. To exalt your own peculiar faith at the expense of the belief of others within the Great Church, is to me self-contradictory and injurious rather than an aid to the accentuated belief that one is trying to promote. It is a happy thing that there are not many preachers who pursue the course of damning the convictions of those who differ from them. The truth wins by its inherent beauty, and constructive preaching and teaching is that which the world today craves more than anything else—the truth about God in His relationship with men, the truth about men in their relationship with Him and with one another. Is there anything more irritating than to find critically minded men saying that society can be saved only by adherence to untried or partially tried theories? If this is their conviction, why do they not lay their life on their aim and prove their theory by their success?

The Church is the Body of Christ. We by virtue of our relationship to it inherit the life that is in Christ. His love encompasses us. His life vivifies us. His light illumines us. So that we can say: "I can do all things through Christ who strengtheneth me."

The Church is essentially social. It therefore demands social expression in organic form. Nothing is clearer than that Christ's earlier teaching was of the coming of a Kingdom superior to and transcending all earthly kingdoms, a Kingdom what will have no end, eternal in the heavens. The Church is

not this Kingdom. It is but the symbol and expression of the
Kingdom. To identify the Church with the Kingdom is to
confuse the means with the end. That there will be a City of
God among men some day, who can doubt? But it is in the
building now. In the fragmentary character of Christianity we
have the raw material. It is for us to build it together under
the superintendence of the Holy Spirit who is the Spirit of
Unity.

The qualities required for the building of God's great temple
are summed up in the Beatitudes which, though somewhat
cryptic, have the intriguing character of all veiled utterances.
Patient meditation upon them opens up wide vistas and fills
the soul with a universe that is as resplendent with God as it
is boundless. It is extraordinary how simple Christ made religion, summing it up in two sentences— "Thou shalt love the
Lord Thy God. . . . Thou shalt love thy neighbor. . . ."—
and how intricate the Christian Church seems to have made it.

My solemn conviction born of years of pain and struggle,
confirmed as I skirt eternity, is that what I have said in the
foregoing pages must form the main background for the truly
Christian life. It is the kernel of the matter. All else, however
important, is of a subordinate nature. If you have, in a sincere
soul, as your permanent ideal, the great principles upon which
I have touched and if you pursue them with "terrible meek-
ness," you will accomplish a work greater than that of empire
builders or world statesmen. It is the within-ness that counts.
It is a new and triumphant phase of this within-ness in human
life for which I yearn. No one can deny it. It is when the
manner and the means are discussed that controversy and
mutual exclusiveness begin. It is not for me to declare in dog-
matic language what the final constitution of the Great Church

will be. Loyalty to the moral and spiritual contents of the communion of our immediate allegiance, provided it be pursued in constructive terms, must contribute to the grand whole of the Church of Christ and help to bring in the Kingdom of God. Public worship, with such thoughts as we have been considering, demands the most careful consideration that human life can give it. It is worship rather than preaching upon which the Church of God should center its attention. Reverent worship is in itself the highest form of teaching. He who does not know how to worship cannot preach, even if he have the tongue of angels. Worship is a task which demands the highest artistic sense, the greatest love of beauty, the highest form of expression, the most appealing method of presentation, of which man is capable. Again let me say that clothed in the principles I have enunciated, principles that are not my own but born of God and fostered through the ages, everything else will come in due order. Without these principles our life and ministry must be barren and the fruit of our work dust and ashes. With them we can see by faith the heavenly Jerusalem descending from God and gathering mankind into its saving embrace.

· 2 ·

"That They All May Be One . . ." [1]

It is the purpose of Jesus Christ to unify the Church. Unity, visible and invisible, is not an accident of the Gospel. It is the Gospel. Only he who labors for unity can perceive and teach the whole Gospel. A fragment can suggest the whole. It cannot reveal it.

The unity of Christendom is not a luxury but a necessity. The world will go limping until Christ's prayer that all may be one is answered. We must have unity, not at all costs, but at all risks. A unified Church is the only offering we dare present to the coming Christ, for in it alone will He find room to dwell.

Do not be deceived; without unity the conversion of great nations is well-nigh hopeless. The success of missions is inextricably bound up with unity. It would seem that missionary progress in the future will depend mainly upon the Church's unity, and that national conversions can be brought about by no other influence.

God has used, beyond anything we had a right to expect,

[1] This chapter is made up of quotations from the Bishop's diaries, addresses, and sermon notes.

38

our divided Christendom. But now that we know the sin and disaster of sectarianism, we cannot hope that He will use it much longer. Sectarianism, in spirit and in form, is *par excellence* the cult of the incomplete. It is a refusal to consider truth and life in terms of the whole, not merely the whole of now but the whole of yesterday. It pins its trust to the dicta of a group or the findings of a fixed period. It is content to worship and to defend a conception of God instead of God. It lacks the shape of the Cross which rises vertically as high as God, and stretches right and left to the outermost bounds of humanity. In its extremist form it not only refuses to recognize as acceptable to Christ any group-culture save its own, but it also questions others' right to continue to be. It is precisely this spirit, not in one special Church but in many, which has disrupted Christendom.

It may be that up to the present a divided Church has been used by God for the extension of His Kingdom among men, but we have no guarantee that He will continue to do so. Indeed there are indications that the divided Church has passed the zenith of such power as it has had, and is declining toward desolation. Divided Christendom has had fair trial—it is a failure.

Division is the Achilles' heel of the Christian enterprise. Much of the anguish of soul, of the doubt, of the alienation of men from the Kingdom of God and His righteousness, lies at the door of the broken condition of the Church, her uncatholic temper, and her apathetic acceptance of the divisions which rend her as though they were not her own fault.

If it is a prophecy that the gates of hell shall not prevail against the Church, it is also prophecy that the Church divided against herself will fall. Disorder in the Church is more terrible than feuds in the family or civil war in the State. If war is an evil in national life, it is a thousandfold greater evil in Church life.

If unity has slipped from our grasp, it is the common fault of the Christian world. If it is to be regained it must be by the concerted action of all Christians. Every section has shared in shattering unity. Every section must share in the effort to restore it. To me, the most important movement of the day is that in the direction of unity from whatever angle. There is no room for impatience. It is absurd to expect definite results in so brief a time.

Is the Church to lead in unity? If so, she must begin by unifying herself. It is laughable to think of a warring Church preaching about a world at peace. There is no lesson which the Churches are learning of greater importance than the impotence of our divided Christianity. It is absurd to aim at a united mankind, or even a united Christian civilization, and to be content with a divided Church. A confused Church will be a potent factor in maintaining a confused world. I see no glimmer of hope for permanent and fraternal peace among the nations without at least as permanent and fraternal a peace among the Churches. Unity of heart and hands among the Churches is the sole hope for the Great Peace. As it is with the family of the nations, so must it be with the family of the churches.

There are four main obstacles in the way of promoting unity: first, acquiescence in the broken order; secondly, the sense of security among great dominating Churches like the Church of England, the Roman Catholic Church, and the Orthodox Churches of the East; thirdly, the misuse of the word "Church"; fourthly, substitutes for unity, of which there

are two principal ones called respectively Interdenomination-
alism and Uniformity.

Humbled and awakened the Churches must renew their
search for peace and unity according to God's will. But how?
(1) Not by slurring over honest differences or by slighting
convictions. There is one thing worse than war—saying peace,
peace, where there is no peace. (2) Not for economic reasons.
(3) Not for the sake of ease and convenience.

Labor for unity must lay its claim on every Christian soul.
It will come when it does come, not with observation, but
through the slow process of the mills of God. The Churches
will become the Church when there is in them all mutual
horizontal as well as unified vertical self-giving. The way to
recover unity is to practice fellowship.

Experience has taught me that what is needed for a long
time to come is unsuspicious, friendly, personal touch between
Christian leaders of every opinion, not in order that they may
have joint services or force outward ecclesiastical unity, but
that they may come to understand one another by the only
process that can create mutual understanding. I mean by human fellowship an interchange of living thought for which
even friendly books are no substitute. Christian Unity, which
is a thing of the Spirit and is founded on Christ's twofold law
of love, comes first, antedating ecclesiastical unity, in which
unity of worship is a necessary climax. It is dangerous to
confuse the manufacture of joint services for the sake of their
being joint, with unity.

Must we not do two things—first, train the hearts of all
professing Christians to the recognition of every professing
Christian of whatever denomination or race as a brother beloved without distinction or difference, and secondly, in fre-

quent and frank conference, deliberate on the things pertaining to the Kingdom, sitting loosely to our opinions and sectarian tenets? Nothing but a united Church will be adequate for that which is fast becoming a united world. Today no man is true to Christ who ignores or thinks lightly of the unity of His Church. It is not the practical which first of all moves us to unity. The call comes not from beneath but from above. A split Church can present only a split Christ.

Church Unity will come after Christian Unity. It would not be gain to aim at oneness as an end in itself. Mere oneness would be a sort of saccharine monotony in which differences would not have been reconciled but rather smothered and hidden under a thick coat of sentimentality. Unity, as I understand it, will come as the result of a whole-hearted devotion to a common center, a common vision, and a common purpose. We do not seek for unity in order to come to Christ, but in coming to Christ we are thereby committed to unity according to His mind, and if we fail to find unity we have missed the way.

· 3 ·

Man's Meeting with God

1. THE LIFE OF PRAYER

Glory of the highest type will live as long as dauntless human souls aspire to God, let the world be as matter of fact or as evil as it chooses.

The world just now is sadly in need of better service, but before this can be rendered there must be better prayer. A low standard of prayer means a low standard of character and a low standard of service. Those alone labor effectively among men who impetuously fling themselves upward toward God.

What must be defended is first the fact that God holds fellowship with men. The method comes second. I would, like William Blake, prefer to believe that the intercourse was within and spiritual rather than after a purely human method. It is the reality of the interior fellowship that is important.

The two great prizes of human life are fellowship with God and in Him fellowship with one another. There is no other wealth. The dimensions of fellowship—height: high as God;

breadth: broad as the human race; depth: deep as our capacity.

Why Men Pray

There are but two great realities in the vast universe—the heart of God and the heart of man, and each is ever seeking the other. It is this that makes adventure for God not an experiment, but a certainty. The appeal issuing from man's abysmal need is met by the amplitude of the divine supply.

The thought of God's keeping tryst with us is a winsome thought. When we go to pray, God has already come to the meeting-place. We are never there first. He is indeed more ready to hear than we to pray, more ready to give more than we desire or deserve than we to ask. He comes not with the spirit of toleration but of ardent love. The great thing to remember is that God, being Who He is, is more ready to hear than we to pray, more eager to give than we to receive, more active to find us than we to find Him. God is ever seeking man: His ear is more sensitive to the words, His heart to the desires, of men than the aspen leaf to the summer breeze, than the compass needle to the call of the poles.

The Naturalness of Prayer

Fellowship with the Divine is as normal as fellowship with man.

Humankind cannot be fairly divided into those who pray and those who do not pray, for everybody prays. Prayer is the universal practice of human nature. There is no commoner form of activity. It is not an artificial part of life, but as in-

stinctive and automatic as breathing. It might be said that
the capacity for prayer is the feature which distinguishes man
from monkey or dog.

Active or dormant, the instinct of prayer abides, a faithful
tenant, in every soul. The instinct to pray may be undeveloped,
or paralyzed by violence, or it may lie bed-ridden in the soul
through long neglect; but even so, no benumbed faculty is
more readily roused to life and nerved to action than that of
prayer. The faculty is there; no one is without it. Whether it
expands, and how, is only a question of the will of the person
concerned.

Prayer Is . . .

Prayer is man's side of converse with God; it is speech Godward. Yes, prayer is speech Godward, and worship is man's
whole life of friendship with God, the flowing out, as it were,
of all that tide of emotion and service which is love's best
speech.

The essence of prayer is desire, forming itself into hope and
aspiration, and mounting up into effort, in the direction of
the unattained. Prayer is the address made by human personality to that with which it is desired to establish affiliations.
It is a movement of the whole being which reaches after the
heart's desire.

Prayer is the committal of our way unto the Lord, just as a
deed of trust is the committal of our possessions to those who
can handle them better than we. By living one day with God,
preparation is made for living all days with God.

One may say that the real end of prayer is not so much to get this or that single desire granted, as to put human life into full and joyful conformity with the will of God.

Prayer is love melted into worship.

The Labor of Prayer

It is productive of much mischief to try to make people believe that the life of prayer is easy. In reality there is nothing quite so difficult as strong prayer, nothing so worthy of the attention and the exercise of all the fine parts of a great manhood. On the other hand there is no man who is not equal to the task.

Prayer is quite the most difficult task a man can undertake; but it has this gracious compensation that in no other duty does God lend such direct, face-to-face help. Man may speak wise words about prayer; the Church may bid to prayer; but God alone can unfold to souls the delicate secrets of prayer. The best help is for the hardest duty—the help that comes straight from the Lord.

Let it be clearly understood, then, that though the art of prayer is a universal art it is the most difficult of all. But even so this is not an excuse for discouragement or a justification of spiritual indolence, for a man's best desires are always the index and measure of his possibilities; and the most difficult duty that a man is capable of doing is the duty that above all he should do.

Simplicity and courage are two virtues indispensable for those who covet to pray well. Especially must they be ready to embrace difficulty and court pain—and that through the long stretch of a lifetime.

How to Pray

Aim to see God before you address Him. In the course of time this practice will become an unbidden habit. You can see Him at least as clearly as you can the absent friend with whom you correspond, for the human lineaments are in the Divine.

Pray with your intelligence. Bring things to God that you have thought out and think them out again with Him. That is the secret of good judgment. Repeatedly place your pet opinions and prejudices before God. He will surprise you by showing you that the best of them need refining and some the purification of destruction.

The difficulty that so many persons find in praying without the aid of some form of devotion is largely due to the impression that the language needed for address to God is not such as an ordinary mortal can frame. There are four leading principles, the first of which contradicts this misconception, that stand out in bold prominence in the Lord's Prayer, and tell us what all speech Godward should be. (1) Prayer must be familiar yet reverent. (2) Prayer should be comprehensive yet definite. (3) Prayer should be social rather than individual in spirit. (4) Prayer must maintain proper proportions.

Though we may have learned the fundamental principles of prayer from devout friends and teachers, whatever we really know of prayer we have learned by praying. Even the mother, at whose knee the earliest phrases of prayer were lisped out, at the best only led us gently into the presence of God. It is not too much to say that the Church herself cannot do more than put the soul very near God and leave it there, trusting that something will come of it. The rest must proceed in direct course from the lips of the Most High Himself. So delicate and subtle is the correspondence between the soul and God, so "intensely personal" a thing is prayer, that we are often seriously hindered rather than helped by the blundering but well-intended efforts of those who would guide us to better devotion. Indeed happy are those souls who have always been able to speak with a reverent yet free familiarity with God, having nothing to aid save the vision of His face.

Answer to Prayer

No prayer ever rises in vain. It is as inevitably answered as is the call of gravitation to matter. Prayer and its answer belong to an established, immovable order, and work according to recognized law. If prayer is manifestly and magnificently answered, we marvel: whereas we should marvel if it is not abundantly answered.

Our steady, simple prayers never fail to reach God. The mere knowledge of that rests one's soul. The consciousness that God has a purpose for each of us and that He will unfold it to us with the eagerness and joy of a lover offering a gift to his bride, is enough to allay if not to kill anxiety. The purpose may not always be clear to us but its golden thread runs through all our days.

A recognition of answer to prayer leads to fresh activity of faith. It is astonishing how even a little progress in our walk by faith opens up the landscape. Victory always leads to victory, progress to progress, prayer answered to prayer to be answered. Beauty that we never dreamed of lies just around that turn of the road; obstacles, which at an earlier stage of our development would have routed us, appear only to be routed.

Prayer must sooner or later melt into thanksgiving as petition is crowned by answer.

God never tells man what man can find out for himself, as He never does what man can do for himself.

God has direct answers to prayer for every soul that appeals to Him. But many fail to recognize the answer when it comes because of inattention. If God is to be heard when He speaks we must give heed. It is no less a duty to "wait still upon God" than it is to address Him in prayer. A one-sided conversation is not a conversation at all. Conversation requires an interchange of thought. He who is one moment the speaker must the next become the listener, intent upon the words of his companion. The expectation of an answer to prayer is laid down as a condition of there being one.

Oftentimes God's answer is in the shape of an action rather than a voice. But when occasion requires, the reply to speech Godward comes in the shape of a voice. In one sense God is always speaking; He is never still. Just as in prayer it is not we who momentarily catch His attention but He ours, so when we fail to hear His voice it is not because He is not speaking so much as that we are not listening. A man must not stop listening any more than praying when he rises from his knees. No one questions the need of times of formal address to God, but few admit in any practical way the need of quiet waiting upon God, gazing into His face, feeling for His hand, listening for His voice. "I will hearken what the Lord God will say concerning me." God has special confidences for each soul. Indeed, it would seem as though the deepest truths came only in moments of profound devotional silence and contemplation.

The written Word of God has special messages for the individual as well as a large general message for the entire Christian body. The devotional use of Holy Scripture is the means by which the soul reaches some of the most precious manifestations of God's will. By devotional use is meant such a study as has for its ultimate purpose an act of worship, or of conscious fellowship with Him.

A third way in which God makes His will known to man is by His silences, silences which are always eloquent. As experience has taught us, silence can convey a message just as readily as speech sometimes, or even more readily. The silence of the Easter tomb was the first voice that told of the Resurrection. God is never silent except when silence speaks more clearly than a voice.

So the sure response comes to speech Godward in an action, or a voice, or a speaking silence. The persevering, faithful, attentive soul will never fail to discern God's answer to prayer, nor be disappointed in the quality of that answer when it comes. God is more ready to hear than we to pray, and it is His wont to give more than either we desire or deserve.

What to Pray For

The sure test of whether it is legitimate to pray for this or that is whether we can carry our desire to the Father of our Lord Christ.

Pray for those who are likely to oppose you or to give you small support. It will prevent the possibility of your life being embittered by their performances whatever they may be. Prayer illumines what is obscure, mollifies pain, banishes vindictiveness and ill will.

None know how to pray for spiritual gifts like the spiritually-gifted. Those who have won wealth by prayer are the ones who are the most conscious of their own poverty and of wealth unachieved.

Intercessory Prayer

Intercession is the soul of service. It gives spiritual meaning to that which we do for others; it makes plain to us just how and where we can best help our fellows; and it furnishes us with a sympathy for and an insight into human life that can be produced through no other channel. It may end in making us poor in pocket, in sending us on some hazardous errand to the needy, or in creating the spirit of adventure for God that will lift us into the uttermost parts of the earth. But its compensation is the bestowal upon its user of an enriched manhood and a tender heart. What spiritual and hidden agencies are let loose by intercession upon those who are prayed for it is hard to determine; but we know, without understanding how or why, that powerful influences for good are released by this enabling devotion which agitates with new effectiveness the unresting hands of God.

Noon-tide is intercession time—not exclusively but fittingly. At that moment Christ entered into the most mysterious and unfathomable recesses of the Atonement. It is a natural resting spot, too, from the business of life, wherein we may exchange outer for inner activities, disciplining self-interest by praying for others and their interests.

Intercessory prayer is not a work of extraordinary merit but a necessary element of devotion. It is the simple recognition in worship of the fundamental law of human life that no man lives or dies alone. But intercession rises to sublime heights when it claims the privilege and the power for each child of God to gather up in his arms the whole family to which he belongs, and carry it with its multifold needs and its glorious possibilities into the presence of the common Father for blessing and protection. It is grand to feel that the Christian can lift, by the power of prayer, a myriad as easily as one, that he can hold in his grasp the whole Church as firmly as a single parish, and can bring down showers of blessing on an entire race as readily as the few drops needed for his own little plot.

The Christ-spirit is the spiritual ether binding man to man as the ether of space binds world to world. Prayer is no mere individual or local act: it is a potent energy that agitates the whole universe of presences as often as it is set in operation. It creates, extends and intensifies presence, unhindered by the mathematics of time or distance. It is a phase of the communion of saints in volitional activity. Prayer in Christ can never be less than intercessory in its direction, for the Christian self can never move without reference to others—first in the broad impulse of life and afterward in its separate details. There is nothing so exquisitely and increasingly sensitive as the Christ fellowship or body. In Christ all things are ours, whether persons or the world or life or death or things present or things to come: all are ours; and we are Christ's; and Christ is God's.

Prayer for others is the most subtle as well as the greatest and deepest force in human society. In its Christian form it is the volitional placing of the power of Christ as we have apprehended, and been apprehended by, Him at the disposal of the individual or the multitude. Every man is present to every man in greater or lesser degree, as we have seen. Prayer establishes the crowning degree of presence. It begins in an act, or series of acts, and ends in a disposition. It is the directive force of our real internal wealth, converting it into a subtle presence advantageous to others, when it is not translated into terms of recognizable service. It does not mean making a passive Christ active in behalf of others, or an unwilling Christ willing, but it means adding my power in Christ to yours. It is affording Him an additional avenue of approach to others. Just as in physics the force of attraction lays hold of every ounce of ponderable matter there is, in order the more completely to influence the rest, so in the volitional spiritual society, the Church, Christ lays hold of each personality, not for its own sake alone, but in order the more completely to exercise influence over and establish presence in the rest. Intercessory prayer is not a scattering of good wishes in the air toward some one we desire to serve; neither is it the vocal or silent emission of pious hopes in the direction of God. It is the orderly operation of a vital energy, an immediate transmitting of life, where the person prayed for is actively receptive, and the creation of fresh opportunity for him, whatever his temper of mind. By the force of spiritual projection, which eliminates space by ignoring it, I lay my life over against that of my friend, simultaneously establishing definite and conscious contact with God. Presence is thereby intensified in both directions, Manward and Godward, and my life becomes more open for God's use as a social vehicle for the bestowal of His gifts. Intercessory prayer makes personality a sacrament. Prayer intensifies the Christ presence in those we pray for. Further it must perforce draw taut the cord that binds men, making presence, visible and invisible, increasingly intimate, and friendship a glory superior to the clouds of misunderstanding and the sins of unfaithfulness. This is a principle quite intelligible to any one who thinks. I speak of a fact, not a theory. Life passes into life through specialized physical contacts—the touch of the nurse, the transfusion of blood. Volitional spiritual presence is at any rate no less powerful than volitional physical presence of the intense sort indicated. Following this analogy it would appear as though we can become agents of power for others, only so far as we ourselves are struggling up to the moral and spiritual heights which we covet for others. A truthful man becomes a vehicle which God can use to aid an untruthful man to become truthful. It is only the self-restrained life that can pray effectually for the unrestrained life. Otherwise no new avenue for God's controlling power to flow is presented, only a desire is expressed that another should receive that which the petitioner himself implicitly at least rejects. The injunction to sanctify ourselves for the sake of others, that they too may be sanctified, thus takes on a new and inspiring meaning. By prayer we are enabled to offer our strength in Christ, or Christ's strength through us, to our fellows.

Results of a Life of Prayer

The most comfortable result of a life of prayer is the security which fellowship with God imparts. His kind and cheering counsels come darting into the soul like rays of light into a dark room. Good desires increase in multitude and vigor. Unlooked-for succor rushes in to support us in moments of trial. Life expands until its branches are aflame with the sunny blossoms of hope.

Probably the greatest result of the life of prayer is an unconscious but steady growth into the knowledge of the mind of God and into conformity with His will; for after all prayer is not so much the means whereby God's will is bent to man's desires as it is that whereby man's will is bent to God's desires.

Our constant appeal to the King so works upon our personality as to make it possible for Him to control our destinies to our fullest benefit.

He who in the ordinary course of everyday life makes nearness to God, companionship with Him, his chief goal, when trouble comes will be given entrance into the sojourning place of God on earth and will find secret doors into God's mysteries. New intimacy with God will spring up and a strong, permanent foundation will be builded for our feet.

The Church at Prayer

The power of public worship is dependent upon and is the outcome of healthy and faithful private worship. Those who have true personal religion will feel their life of devotion incomplete without common prayer; a growing desire for public worship is an index of a man's deepening spirituality. On the other hand, when we hear men saying that they do not care for church services, that they can pray just as well at home, and so on, it is safe to conclude that whatever fine-spun theories they may hold, as a matter of fact they are suffering from spiritual atrophy, praying neither at home nor anywhere else. Private devotion whets the appetite for public worship. And those who are in intention true to fundamental Christian principles will not mistake the end of the Church's corporate worship.

The assembling of the congregation is something far larger than the creation of a public occasion for saying private prayers. There are numbers of persons who go through the whole service without a thought for any one but themselves, sucking the liturgy dry of whatever touches their own immediate concerns, but oblivious to those who kneel around; and perhaps private manuals supply the place of the Prayer Book. Such persons squeeze into their own cup all the inspiration that a harmonious concourse of men carries with it, and make no return. Like the horse-leach's daughters their cry is, "Give, give." Could anything be more selfish or more anomalous? There is no effort of imagination, no kindling of sympathy, no struggle to enter under the shadow of the prayer of the congregation, so that they are as completely alone as though they were in a desert place.

Nor is public worship a device for rousing in people a devotional frame of mind, which will enable them to pray better by themselves. Doubtless one indirect effect of the great dignity and beauty of liturgical worship, is to stimulate those who participate in it to a deeper devotion at home. But public worship is a climax, not a mere means to an end; it is the culmination of private devotion, not its starting point. Without hidden spiritual effort, it is a phantom of the real thing; with it, it is the matchless consummation of adoration, prayer and sympathy. Under the least satisfactory conditions the congregation gathered in God's house has marvellous dignity; the unity of movement, the rich variety and the rhythm of liturgical expression characterize it as the most august of human assemblies.

But the possibilities of the Church in prayer rise to their supremest height, when the congregation is rich with the fruits of personal religion. So closely woven are the public and the private phases of devotion that they are of a piece. The power of the former is due to the house of secret prayer, the struggles with self, the nerving of the will—in short, all that hidden discipline and training that lie behind the veil of private life. Out of this, corporate worship emerges as effect rises out of cause. However great, then, the private life of devotion is in which men pray to God in the guarded secrecy of their homes, it is only preparatory, leading up to the service of the sanctuary. Private prayer is the lesser, public the greater; the former is the exercise of the individual members with special regard to their own development, the latter is the stately movement of the whole body in beautiful unison. Each member contributes to the whole what has been gained in private efforts; each comes to give rather than to receive, or, if it may be so put, to receive through giving; and of course a man can give only what he has gathered.

The glimpses we have of heavenly worship reveal nothing but common worship. We see no individuals standing apart from the throng, absorbed in their own little expression of praise. The ranks are unbroken, and one united and uniting impulse thrills the whole. The visions recorded by St. John are visions not merely of ideal worship in its restricted sense of spoken prayer and praise, but of the ideal life. The fundamental idea of common worship consists in dependence upon God and fellowship with man, and when all life is filled to the full with this twofold spirit, all life will be worship, and let it be said here with firm emphasis, that if we do not lift up our life to the level of our prayers, eventually our prayers will be dragged down to the level of our life. Life in heaven is something more than one long Sunday service; it is the use of all powers and faculties in the spirit of worship, worship representing the highest and finest temper of mind of which we have experience. So when we read the figurative language of St. John, we must remember that he is declaring under the symbolism of worship what the features of heavenly life are— the conscious service of God in a harmonious human society.

Similarly here on earth common worship is a symbol of true life as well as a means of sustaining it. The attention of the congregation gathered before the altar is fixed upon God, and no stronger indication of the reality of brotherhood could be conceived than the visible assembly occupied in a common exercise. When all our activities become saturated with the consciousness of God in His perfection, and with the fact of the oneness of Christ's mystical Body, formal worship will be no more a necessity. But that will be when heaven is reached, for

which day there must be some little waiting yet. In the meantime it is vital that worship, as we know it, should not be an
excrescence on life but a real part of it, part of it as truly as the
deep, silent tide flowing between narrow banks is part of the
same river which above and below is worried by rocks or
widened into a lake. Public worship should represent perhaps
the most concentrated part of life, but nothing unnatural,
nothing out of gear with work-a-day moments. Work should
flow into worship as easily as the stream into the ocean.

Again, public worship ought to be the highest and not the
only expression of parochial family life. The assembled congregation is the symbol of an enduring Christian brotherhood,
where mutual consideration, love and service form the unalterable watchwords. Today this thought is much obscured
by the parochial family having so little reality outside the
church walls. This is especially applicable to city churches,
where congregations gather from the remotest localities. The
parish seems to be fast dying out and the congregation is
taking its place. The people who worship in the same building
neither know one another nor in many instances, desire to.
This is simply fatal to ideal public worship, one purpose of
which at any rate is to quicken and seal the sympathy that
already exists as the result of intercourse in the outside world.

The use of a liturgy is an added power to public worship.
Left to themselves men lose the true perspective of things; they
dwell too much on matters of secondary importance, and become insular in their outlook. A liturgy comes in as a correc-
tive of these constitutional failings; it confronts us with all that
is vast in the realm of truth; it calls us away from the consideration of those things over which we have pondered until
morbidness has seized upon us; it ministers that grateful rest

which comes from the mind being freed from the contemplation of one set of interests, by being caught away by and absorbed in new and wider interests; it rounds out the devotional life; it invites us to lean upon the prayers of others as we desire them to lean on ours.

Demeanor in the congregation is a small thing to think of after the great central theme that has been holding our attention. But nothing is unworthy of consideration which bears on the perfecting of common worship; and two simple observations on demeanor remain to be mentioned. First, regarding the self-consciousness that both distresses the soul and weakens its devotional power. The sense, while in the act of prayer, of being observed by others, is distracting. But is it not a piece of conceit to imagine that we are being observed, widely at any rate, as well as something akin to an insult to those about us? Are we not implicitly charging them with neglect of duty and with irreverence? After all they are probably occupied with their devotions as we ourselves should be. The simplest way of conquering the distraction when it arises is to take the person or persons concerned into our prayers by a conscious act. Then in the second place, as to our own behavior, it is only common charity to avoid singularity of conduct. Most of the ordinary acts of reverence which the individual may practice, can be so unobtrusively performed as not to attract notice. But when there is a danger of causing distraction to others, as in a strange parish for instance, it is more conducive to real reverence to omit than to observe them. Sometimes the best way to be loyal to a principle is deliberately to break a rule, and if this suggestion be reasonable then why should not a person, unaccustomed to ornate ritual, fall in with any

legitimate customs observed, if he finds himself at any time
in a church where such customs obtain?

2. PRAYERS FOR PERSONAL NEEDS

On Waking

The day must begin with a cheerful outlook. Hope is the
gift of the dawn. With the breaking of the day the powers of
evil falter and flee. There is no moment of time so free from
sin as when the sun first touches the East.

Opportunity opens wide its gates to me as I renew consciousness with the day. Contentment is the result of discerning the
value of the things we have and the conditions that enfold
us. If the evil of the day is sufficient thereunto, so is the joy.
The gladness most worth having is that which is at hand growing by today's highway. Pluck it: it will be a present delight
and a future treasure in memory's storehouse.

O Heavenly Father, our Lover and Creator, in whom we
live and move and have our being, at whose touch darkness
gives place to light and night to day, lay Thy morning hand
on all our faculties which sleep and fill them with the light of
Thy life that we may rejoice in the performance of the hard
tasks which are the portion of strong men.

O Light of the world, who daily enterest our conscious life
on the wings of the dawn, illumine our minds this day with
wisdom and our hearts with joy, that, being defended by the
brightness of Thy countenance from the darkness of sin, we
may radiate Thy gracious influence among our fellow men

to the purification of human life and the glory of Thy great name.

O God, who hast folded back the black mantle of the night to clothe us in the golden glory of the day, chase from our hearts all gloomy thoughts and make us glad with the brightness of hope, that we may effectively aspire to unwon virtues; through Jesus Christ our Lord.

Lord of the dawn, dispel the darkness of our hearts by the light of Thy truth as we reverently approach Thy glorious presence. Reveal to us day by day the path of eternal life, that with settled purpose and single mind we may pursue an unfaltering course until night falls and we are received into safe lodging with Thee who givest Thy beloved sleep.

O God, Who givest Thy spirit without measure to those who prepare for Him a dwelling, make us worthy temples of His presence, that, our souls and bodies being swept clean of evil and adorned with virtue, we may joyfully welcome the heavenly guest in His full splendor to the sanctification of our lives; through Jesus Christ our Lord.

O God, the wonders of whose being rise above our minds in regal splendor, we bow in awed reverence before Thy divine majesty and worship Thee who art past understanding. Knowing Thee (not as Thou knowest us) but dimly as in a mirror, we thank Thee for the abundant self-showing of Thyself in the face of Jesus Christ. Let the clear flame of Thy love in our hearts so kindle in us responsive love that we may more and more know Thee as Thou art in all the brightness and beauty of Thy glory; through Jesus Christ our Lord.

O Word of God who givest us our thoughts that we may speak them back to Thee, we offer Thee this day the first fruits of our hearts and minds beseeching Thee to heed our loftiest aspirations, and to grant that, as they have come from Thee as promptings, so they may return to Thee as righteous deeds, carrying on high our wills made captive to Thy wisdom.

O God, open my eyes to see, cleanse my life to do, nerve my courage to bear, all that Thy will wills for me. Grant me to love, to rejoice, to be tranquil, to be pure, to be true, to trust, so that before I go hence and be no more seen I may be known by Thee as a loyal and loving bondservant of Thine and of those who are Thine.

Draw our affections, Lord, up to the heights where Thou dwellest, that, our hearts being set not on things seen but on things unseen, our lives may be shaped according to Thy pattern and filled with the vision of Thy beauty.

The Daily Walk

God asks us for a day-long effort—"keep us this day without sin." My main motive in life must be (1) to seek, (2) to do, God's will. Some things are obvious. Implicit obedience to them clears the eye to see deeper duties, refinements of duty. The day must be begun early, with prayer leading to action.

The real difficulty in life is to keep the spirit active in its upward efforts. The daily cultivation of the interior virtues, so attractive in contemplation, calls for one's best endeavor and constant vigilance.

To recognize and obey the voice of Christ is as necessary as prayer. If each day we were to identify some clear call to righteousness with His voice, it would not be long before His person and guidance were the dominant reality in life.

O God, who orderest the common things of the common day, dignify by Thy presence and aid the trivial round and routine tasks of Thy servant whose hope is in Thee, that least duties may be grandly done and all activities marked with the seal of Thy righteousness; through Jesus Christ our Lord.

O Christ, our Brother, who in this very flesh hast reached the land where joy and service are one, lead us thither, that where Thou art there may we also be. Teach us heirs of mortality how to practice immortality in our daily walk, that in the midst of death we may ever be in life. Help us to claim as present wealth the glorious things to be, the battles won and tasks complete, that we may rejoice in hope and by faith give substance to the glory of the unseen.

Valiant Lord, who in our very nature didst fight to win and labor to achieve, clothe us with Thy valor, that we of Thy household being delivered from the fear of living as Christians, may unite as comrades in service to attack the problems of our troubled day, with serene mind and victorious will, till our last foe is vanquished and our last task finished to Thy honor and glory, who livest and reignest God for evermore.

Endue us, O God, with such a measure of patience as will enable us to win our lives, that we may never, "even for one moving moment, lose that complete possession of ourselves which is the first condition of good service."

Give us, Lord, lofty ambition such as will be satisfied with nothing less than the noble best and nothing short of the goal of final reality, that we may come to know the truth and that the truth may make us free; through Him who is the Way, the Truth, and the Life, Jesus Christ.

Grant us, Lord, the will to live Christianly, that by Thy might we may storm the fortress of evil and set free its prisoners into the glorious liberty of the children of God.

O God, who hast proclaimed the victorious destiny of man by Thyself achieving it in human form, give us the will to win the battle of life that we may find strength in weakness, quiet in turbulence and triumph in failure; through Jesus Christ our Lord.

Be very near to us, Lord, in the abundance of Thy life, that Thy wisdom may be our guiding light, Thy righteousness the goal of our effort, Thy strength the armor of our warfare; through Jesus Christ our Saviour.

Help us, Heavenly Father, so to gain control of our minds that we may always direct our thoughts to do Thy bidding, and that whatsoever things are true, whatsoever things are honorable, whatsoever things are just, whatsoever things are pure, whatsoever things are lovely, whatsoever things are of good report; if there be any virtue, and if there be any praise, we may think on these things.

Heavenly Father, deliver us Thy children from the slavery of things and enlighten us with Thy Spirit that we may choose the glorious liberty of the sons of God, that looking not at the things which are seen but at the things which are unseen, we may claim Thy promises which exceed all that we can desire; through Jesus Christ our Lord.

O God, source of all wisdom, unite us in a common purpose to seek and to know the truth as revealed in Christ, that companying with one another in our pilgrimage Godward, we may together attain that perfect knowledge of Thee in which standeth our eternal life; through Jesus Christ our Lord.

Lord, lift us out of private-mindedness and give us public souls to work for Thy Kingdom by daily creating that atmosphere of brotherhood by a happy temper, a friendly mind and a generous heart, which alone can bring in the Great Peace to Thy honor and the comfort of mankind.

Heavenly Father, Who in the richness of Thy love invitest us men into conscious fellowship with Thee, grant that we may find Thy mystic presence in the Church's solemn assembly where we gather to adore Thee in the wonder of Thy beauty, in the splendor of Thy truth, and in the joy of Thy loving kindness, revealed in Thy Son Jesus Christ our Lord.

Lord Jesus, who didst stretch out Thine arms of love on the hard wood of the Cross, that all men might come within the reach of Thy saving embrace, clothe us in Thy Spirit, that we, stretching forth our hands in loving labor for others, may bring those who know Thee not to the knowledge and love of Thee, who with the Father and the Holy Ghost livest and reignest one God.

At Night

The kind of night we spend is in a large degree for us to determine. The Christian should at times leave everything in God's hands, and do nothing but lie back on God's bosom. The opportunity comes every night when we go to sleep. This is the season when the mind and soul should rest not less than the body. We can train ourselves to shed our cares into God's arms if we try. So far from gaining anything we lose much by submitting to wakefulness begotten of anxiety. Anxiety gnaws at the cords of good judgment and leaves us with a warped mind when the day dawns after a troubled night. Sweet sleep delights to respond to the invitation of a peaceful conscience and a mind whose last thoughts sway to and fro in the cradle of God's love. A trustful consideration of God's care of our concerns is frequently the only sleep-giving medicine necessary for distraught nerves.

Eternal Father, who alone canst control the days that are gone and the deeds that are done, remove from my burdened memory the weight of past years, that, being set free both from the glamor of complacency and the palsy of remorse, I may reach forth unto those things which are before and press toward the mark for the prize of the high calling of God in Christ Jesus.

very good

Lord, give me the repentance which is of the will, that, not only in desire but also in intention and effort I may embrace what is good, especially those virtues which once I neglected or refused, and so be endued with power to accept Thy pardon; through Jesus Christ our only Mediator and Advocate.

O God, who requirest of me only such things as will turn to my profit, and who art pained by my least act of waywardness, warm my heart until it is aflame with love toward Thee, that my chief delight may be to bring Thee joy by my fidelity to Thy counsels; through Jesus Christ our Lord.

O God of man, who hast brought us through the difficulties and dangers of life, be with us yet until we die. We have done wrong and need Thy forgiveness. Make us clean where we are stained, and strong where we are weak. Help us to lay hold of our various tasks with willing hands and cheerful faces, and to do them with thoroughness. Inspire us with respect for ourselves and for one another, that we may be worthy of Thy regard.

O God, who wast the brightness of the dawn's first rays and of the noontide's glory, according to Thy most sure promise fail not to give us light at evening time. Dispel by Thy pardoning love the gloom of this day's guilt, and through the hours of darkness keep bright in our souls the star of trust in Thy sheltering care; through Jesus Christ our Lord.

very good

O God, who hast drawn over weary day the restful veil of night, wrap our consciences in heavenly peace. Lift from our hands our tasks, and all through the night bear in Thy bosom the full weight of our burdens and sorrows, that in untroubled slumber we may press our weakness close to Thy strength, and win new power for the morrow's duty from Thee who givest Thy beloved sleep.

O God, whose guiding hand has until now led me safely *very good* through the changes of this world, be with me at the close of my work as Thou wast with me at the beginning. Though my faith has been feeble and my efforts faint, Thou hast never failed me. Abide with me as the day wanes, and give me a resting-place near Thy feet, when the night falls; through Him who turns sorrow into joy and darkness into light, Jesus Christ our Lord.

3. PRAYERS FOR OCCASIONS AND CAUSES

For Children

Look with favor, Heavenly Father, on little children everywhere. Defend them from the unkindness of men and all evil influences; and make us like to them, that with them we may enter the Kingdom of Heaven; through Jesus Christ our Lord.

For a Children's Corner

Grant Thy blessing, Lord, to this place where little children whom Thou dost love are wont to gather to talk with Thee. Be present in Thy love and favor with all who kneel here. Make Thyself known to them. Hear their prayers and make them true followers of Thine; through Jesus Christ our Lord.

For Young People

Father, we praise Thee for the young, for those about to live. Give them souls of flame to search Thy counsels, and wills of steel to do Thy will. Make them honest workmen that they may work diligently while it is day. Refine their taste and correct their manners, that their leisure may be undefiled by unworthy recreation or their beauty marred by lawless pleasure. Furnish them with wings of love that they may surely and swiftly reach the heights of service, to the glory of Thy great Name and the benefit of mankind; through Jesus Christ our Lord.

For a Boys' School

Lord Jesus, who understandest the boy's heart, for Thou too were once a boy, we take Thee to be our Leader. Remember now Thy boyhood days and help us to master our temptations and realize our ideals. Make us lovers of our homes, loyal to our country, faithful to our God. Keep clean as a flame of fire the inner world of the heart, that our motives may be pure, our thoughts honorable, our desires manly. Encourage us to rejoice in measuring our youthful strength with hard tasks, till duty mounts into privilege and struggle into victory. Heed our aspirations; and grant that as they come from Thee as promptings, so they may return to Thee as righteous deeds, carrying on high our wills made captive to Thy service, who art the Way, the Truth, and the Life, now and ever.

For a College Graduating Class

Father, we, Thy sons, gather at the beginning of our festival day to offer Thee our gratitude for having given us unremitting guidance and protection throughout the course of our college life, now at its close. Thou hast borne with our limitations, forgiven our moral lapses, and enlightened our ignorances. Be favorable to us now while we renew our pledge of loyalty to Thee and Thy teachings as we stand on the threshold of life's serious business. Enfold us with the girdle of moral purity which will ten-fold increase our strength. Give us truth in the inward parts that, ridding our souls of all insincerity and deceit, we may contribute to enduring knowledge. Help us to keep inviolate our ideals that, with tireless patience and invincible courage, we may not flag in the battle of life but fight till we win. Clothe us in divinest self-forgetfulness that in our most troubled moments we may know the peace and happiness that pass all understanding. We ask Thy blessing on our Alma Mater that she may be prospered in all her undertaking and adventures for the sake of the truth that sets men free.

For Benefactors

Be pleased, O Lord, to remember all those, our friends, whose gifts have enriched us. Do Thou good to them, and return all their kindness double into their own bosom, rewarding them with blessings, and sanctifying them with Thy graces, and bringing them to glory; through Jesus Christ our Lord.

For Ideals in Business Life

Lord and Master Workman of the universe, who hast committed to us the swift and solemn trust of life, we thank Thee for our task of weaving the threads of human affairs into the fabric of Thy purpose. Clothe us with wisdom in our stewardship as we drive the shuttle of commerce from man to man and nation to nation. May the spirit of righteousness be our guide through the entire stretch of life, in home and club, in office and factory, in work and leisure, that we may never value things above men, or surrender honor to the love of gain or the lust of power. Prosper all efforts to put an end to toil that brings no joy, and teach us how to govern the ways of industry to the hurt of none and to the benefit and prosperity of the commonwealth.

For Doctors

O Lord, the healer of all our diseases, who knowest how the sick have need of a physician, bless all whom Thou hast called to be sharers in Thine own work of healing with health alike of body and soul, that they may learn their art in dependence upon Thee and exercise it always under Thy sanction and to Thy glory, who liveth and reigneth God forever and ever.

For Nurses

O Good Jesus, who hast said, "Inasmuch as ye do it unto the least of these my brethren, ye do it unto me," look upon Thy servants who have been called by Thee to tend Thy sick and suffering children. Give them patience and tenderness, wisdom and truthfulness, and the special guidance of Thy Holy Spirit in their work, so that they may faithfully minister to those to whom Thou shalt send them, in Thee and for Thee, and may be found worthy, at the last, to receive Thy eternal reward; for Thine own merit's sake.

For Hospital Patients

Good Jesus, physician of souls and bodies, make all sickness a healing medicine to the soul; soothe by Thy presence each ache and pain; hallow all suffering by Thine all-holy sufferings, and teach sufferers to unite their sufferings with Thine, to be hallowed by Thine. Look mercifully upon them and, after that they have suffered a little while, make them perfect, stablish, strengthen, and settle them. Hear our prayer, O Saviour, who by Thy Cross and Passion hast redeemed us.

For the Family

Shed the bright rays of Thy light, O Father, upon this family and household, that every member of the same, made confident by Thy guidance, may fulfill his daily duty with pure motive and gallant heart. Be close to us in times of stress and strain, that our courage and our hope may never fail. Let Thy sheltering arm protect us, that we may be valiant in all peril. Turn Thou for us sorrow into joy, darkness into sunshine, death into life, so that when evening comes and our work on earth is done we may pass triumphantly into the up-lands of fellowship in Thy family above; through Jesus Christ our Lord.

For All Dear Ones

Father, grant to my dear ones all the best gifts Thou hast ever bestowed on me, and, adding bounty to bounty, enlarge Thy favor so as to flood their lives with treasures and blessings beyond my understanding to know or my merits to receive; through Him who, being rich, became poor that we through His poverty might become rich, even Thy Son Jesus Christ our Lord.

For Loved Ones Departed

O King of Paradise, where light abounds and life reigns, give to our dear ones who are with Thee a full share of Thy treasures, that they may always be white with Thy purity, tranquil with Thy peace, and glad with Thy joy. Let us live vividly in their present love as they live in ours, until the time of separation is past, and we are taken to the place whither they have gone before, there to dwell with them in the perfect fellowship that knows no end.

At the Lord's Table

O Christ of the Eucharist, who in a special manner dost manifest Thyself to Thy people in the Sacrament of Thy body and blood, make Thyself known to us in the breaking of the Bread, that by faith we may clearly see Thy form and humbly adore Thy presence, who art God forever and ever.

O Christ of the Passion, who at the Last Supper didst bequeath to the Church a perpetual memorial of the sacrifice of the Cross, help us in this holy Sacrament stedfastly to contemplate Thy redeeming love, that we may ever be mindful of the price wherewith Thou hast bought us; who livest and reignest with the Father and the Holy Ghost, ever one God, world without end.

O Living Bread, that camest down from heaven to give abundant life to the world in this Sacrament of the holy food, feed us with Thy body and Thy blood, that we may live in Thy life, labor in Thy strength, and inherit Thy joy; who livest and reignest, God, world without end.

Grant, O Son of God, that as Thou and the Father are one, so we Thy people may be bound together in Thee. Unite in mutual forbearance, loyalty, and brotherly kindness, us Thy brethren who are fellow-guests at this Thy table, that we, being moved by the common impulse of Thine eternal purpose, may promote the peace of Thy Kingdom in the daily interminglings of our common life; whom with the Father and the Holy Ghost we worship and glorify as God forever and ever.

For the Grievously Afflicted

Fold in Thy compassion, loving Jesus, those who are smitten with disease. Lay a healing hand upon the wounds of their souls, that inner peace may be their portion. Revive their failing strength and let life conquer death in their suffering bodies, that rejoicing in Thy mercy they may serve Thee with grateful hearts all their days upon earth.

For All Who Mourn

In Thy boundless compassion, O Lord, console all who mourn. Give to them that faith which sees in death but the gate to life eternal, so that with quietude and fearlessness they may continue their course on earth until by Thy call they are united to their loved ones gone before; through Jesus Christ our Lord.

For Blessing on a Sorrowing Friend

O God, let the hand of blessing rest upon Thy servant. Keep him ever constant in the integrity of faith and righteousness. Touch with consoling hand his sorrow. Give him tranquil wisdom in his responsibilities. Accompany him down life's pathway and enable him to ascend on high in heart and mind and with Thee continually dwell; through Jesus Christ our Lord.

For the Church

Almighty God, without whom our labor is but lost, prosper the work of Thy Holy Church throughout the world, O prosper Thou our handiwork. Build it upon that foundation other than which no man can lay, Jesus Christ. Defend it from the defilement of worldly motives, unclean hands and the lust of visible success, that in that day when the fire shall prove each man's work of what sort it is, ours may abide, and we, Thy laborers, have praise of Thee; through the same Jesus Christ our Lord.

For a Diocese

Lord, we the clergy and people of this Diocese offer Thee united praise for Thy past guidance and protection. Be with us now as, at the dawn of a new era, we move forward to meet our new opportunities and perils. Let no problem daunt us, no failure dismay us, no success dazzle us. Build us up in Christian life and worship, that we may promote Thy Kingdom of love and righteousness; through Jesus Christ our Saviour.

For a Blessing on the Churches

O God, who madest the Gospel for a united Church, refuse not, because of our misunderstandings of its message and the dissensions that rend the oneness of Christendom, to continue Thy saving work in the broken order of our making. Bless the labors of all Churches bearing the name of Christ and striving to further righteousness and faith in Him. Show us wherein we are sectarian in our contentions, and give us grace humbly to confess our fault to those whom in past days our Communion has driven from its fellowship by ecclesiastical tyranny, spirit-

ual barrenness, or moral inefficiency, that we may become
worthy and competent to bind up in the Church the wounds of
which we are guilty. Help us to place the truth above our
conception of it, joyfully to recognize the presence of Thy Holy
Spirit wherever He may choose to dwell among men. Endue
us with the mind of Christ, that we may all become one in Him.

For Laborers in the Harvest

O Lover of men, whose pleading voice is never silent in the
souls of men, quicken the dullness of our ears to hear Thy message and obey Thy bidding. Win to Thy following the youth
of our day and separate from them spiritual leaders for the
work whereunto Thou hast called them. Give Thy chosen
servants vivid faith wherewith to know Thee, unfeigned holiness wherewith to exemplify Thee, fiery enthusiasm wherewith
to inflame their fellows, that Thy Church being supplied with
devoted priests and loyal pastors may draw multitudes into
the joy and power of Thy fellowship; through Him Who is the
Chief Shepherd, Jesus Christ.

For Missions and Missionaries

Inflame the Church of our day, O Lord, with love for Thee
and obedience to Thy will, that we may freely give of ourselves
and our substance to the enlightenment of the ignorant, the
conversion of wrong-doers and the building up of Thy Kingdom everywhere. Fill with love, joy and peace our missionaries
at home and abroad, that they may make fruitful barren
places and the desert to blossom as a rose. Increase our laborers, multiply our givers, enlarge our gifts, that we may honor
Thee and win mankind to a sincere following of Christ;
through the same Jesus Christ our Lord.

For Missionaries

O God, who never failest to go with those Thou sendest, bless Thy servants whom Thou hast chosen to bear Thy name before the dwellers in the uttermost part of the earth, that they may have wisdom to know, strength to do, and patience to suffer; through Jesus Christ our Lord.

For a Missionary Conference

O God, who from the beginning didst order and guide the labors of those sent forth to preach Thy word, fail us not who aspire to evangelize the world in this generation. Grant that our deliberations may bear fruit in united effort, wise plans, and quickened love, that the knowledge of the Lord may speedily cover the earth as the waters cover the sea; for the sake of Him who is the light of the world, Jesus Christ our Lord.

For the Unity of the Church

Lord Jesus, whose will it is to fold Thy flock and to make us all one in Thee, behold our earnestness to be gathered into the peace and unity of Thy appointment. Guide us who have lost our way into the path leading to Thee and to Thy purpose. Enable us each and all to find Thee and in Thee to find one another. Bless our efforts to follow Thy counsels and in love to reason together concerning the things that separate, to the end that, misunderstanding and self-seeking and prejudice being dispelled, we may see clearly the blessed goal and in passionate devotion pray and seek and knock until we know as we are known and love as we are loved.

For the Lausanne Conference 1927 He died March 27, 1929,

Bathe with golden showers of blessing, O Lord, Thy servants whom Thy voice is calling into Thy presence to counsel with Thee concerning the peace and unity of the Church of God. Let knowledge prevail over ignorance, goodwill over prejudice, understanding over blindness, that, guided by the Spirit of Truth and Wisdom, we may press onward with joy and confidence toward that happy day when there will be one flock under one Shepherd, Jesus Christ our Saviour.

For Our Country

O Almighty and everlasting God, who, with Thy strong arm and sleepless vigilance, dost govern those nations that look to Thee for guidance, we rejoice in the tokens of Thy favor which have been our portion hitherto and now since our forefathers laid the foundations of this Republic in Thy name. Carry us, we pray Thee, in security to an honorable and glorious destiny; and grant that neither through arrogance begotten of prosperity, nor conceit bred of successful achievement, may we forget our dependence upon Thee for daily sustenance, lest we be cast from Thine embrace into the valley of destruction. To those who sit in the seats of authority impart purity of motive, right judgment in counsel, discretion in administration; to the people of the land grant loyalty, industry and godliness, that all things may tend to the healing of divisions, the establishment of peace, and the promotion of Thy Kingdom among men; through Jesus Christ our Lord.

For All in High Office

Lord, be with all who are burdened with the responsibility of high office. Add the illumination of Thy counsel and wisdom

to their gifts that they may see clearly and choose the right.
Deliver them from self-love that they may be servants of all.
Sustain them in the pressure of daily cares. Give them con-
stancy and stability in the execution of their duties that they
may be true leaders of thy people; through Jesus Christ our
Lord.

For the President of the United States

Almighty God, the fountain of all wisdom, guide and direct,
we beseech Thee, the mind and heart of Thy servant who is
called to exercise the responsibility of President of the United
States. Grant that he may promote Thy will among men, the
temporal and spiritual welfare of our nation, and the peace
of the world. And to those who are chosen to the cabinet give
a right judgment, the spirit of courage and discretion and true
godliness, to the advancement of Thy Kingdom and the benefit
of our people.

Armistice Day

O God and Father of mankind, we gather on this sacred day
to bear solemn testimony before Thee and our fellow men to
our loving gratitude for all those who, at the country's call,
have met the rude shock of battle and have surrendered their
lives amid the ruthless brutalities of war. We pray Thee, Lord,
to grant them safe lodging in heavenly mansions and a holy
rest. Forbid that their sufferings and death should be in vain;
and mercifully vouchsafe that through their devotion the
horrors of war may pass away from the earth and Thy Kingdom of right and honor, of peace and brotherhood, may be
established among men. Comfort, O Lord, we pray Thee, all
who proudly mourn the loss of those near and dear to them,

especially the families of our brothers departed. Support them by Thy love. Give them faith to look beyond the troubles of this present time and to know that neither life nor death can separate us from the Care of God, which is in Christ Jesus our Lord.

The Passion for Peace

O Lord our God, inflame our hearts with such a passion for peace which is born not of our fond desires but of Thy inflexible purpose, that we may avenge the valiant dead by displacing madness by sanity, force by reason, war by law. Raise up in our midst leaders of vision and courage who, scorning peril, will guide our nation into great adventures for the well-being of mankind and the establishment of enduring peace in the whole world. Quell national arrogance wherever it prevails. Frustrate intrigue and selfish scheming. Make goodwill reign in the hearts of men and speedily bring us out of our present confusion into the order and righteousness of Thy Kingdom, through Him Who is Prince of Peace and Saviour, in Whose name and words we pray.

For the Coming of Peace

O God of Nations, who through Thy prophets of old hast foretold a day when the armaments of war shall be beaten into the implements of peace, hasten the fulfillment of this Thy most sure promise. Quell the haughty cries of the nations. Disperse the peoples that delight in war. Speedily release those who are now entangled in the net of mutual destruction and bring us out of our present confusion into the order and righteousness of Thy Kingdom; through Jesus Christ the Prince of Peace, our Saviour.

For the Unity of Mankind

O Father, who art the Maker and Lover of the myriads of men that populate the world, arouse us to a practical belief in the full breadth of our human relationships, that we may rid us of the shackles of sectionalism, national pride, and racial prejudice, and in the spirit of mutual helpfulness combine to establish those conditions of brotherhood and amity which it is our responsibility to promote. Hush the proud boastings of the nations, that they may learn to use their strength, their knowledge, their material greatness to support the weak, to enlighten the ignorant, to enrich the poor. Beat the harsh armaments of war into the kindly implements of industry and peace. Bind together the peoples of East and West by the ties of sympathy, respect and service, that in appreciation and recognition of one another's virtues and with considerate forbearance in our differences, we may be unified into one family according to Thy purpose; through Jesus Christ our Lord.

4. MEDITATIONS

Thy Love

O God, I praise Thee for Thy love, that which Thou art and without which Thou couldst not be the God of man. Thy love controls and shapes Thy power so that Thy almighty hand never slips in its creative task but makes all things well. Thy love melts Thy disciplines into the gold of spiritual treasure, and distills the soft rain of compassion from the clouds of trouble. Nothing can escape the transfiguring touch of Thy love. Under its reign the darkness becomes as the light and the unseemly face of evil flees away in shame and defeat. O God, I praise Thee for Thy love which bathes me, even me.

Light in Darkness

It is easy to praise Thee, O God, for the joys that flow from
Thee and for Thy beauty. But in the mystery of Thy control
of life there are dark places which cloud my soul. How can I
make music in my heart for these? Whatever it is it must be
music of faith. The mystery is too deep for me to plumb. But
thou dost not allow evil to reign. Thine is the victory. The very
wrath of man can be turned to Thy praise. Darkness and sorrow and pain may call forth a minor note but even a sobbing
song can praise Thee. Therefore, O God, I praise Thee in
storm and sunshine. Praised be God.

Deserved Suffering

"What glory is it, if, when ye sin, and are buffeted for it, ye
shall take it patiently?" Ay, Lord, why? It is of Thy mercy,
my loving and righteous Judge, that Thou dost not abate my
chastisement. Thy lash is the lash of love, therefore it is my
simple duty to praise Thee even when the ache of punishment
is sore. Sin is disease: punishment is remedy. I praise Thee for
the fitness of all the disciplines which have followed on my
trespasses. Lord, help me not to fear them, but to embrace
them and to kiss the Cross of Thy loving justice. I would pray
Thee for one favour—that the penalties which are wholly
mine may not be visited on others to their hurt. If they too must
share innocently what I bear justly, let mystic power trans-
figure their pain until there comes to them clear shining after
storm. Thus, Lord, do I trust Thee as the dear Avenger of my
sins, and praise Thee for such shame and suffering as is my due
portion.

Discipline

Praise God for His disciplines. It is good for me that I have been in trouble. Thy chastisement has brought me to myself so that I can see the depth and enormity of my sin, and the height and grandeur of Thy forgiving compassion. Thy terrors have I suffered with a troubled mind, but out of the austerities of Thy love have come visions of hope and encouragement. My sin is ever before me, but of Thy mercy as forgiven sin. I praise Thee, my God, that Thou dost show me how bad I am in order that I may see how good I may be. I praise Thee that Thou dost not chastise to destroy but to build up and save to the uttermost. Behold, happy is the man whom God correcteth.

The Joy of Life

All is not dark. There is always sunshine somewhere for which I praise God—the sunshine that brightens other lives when mine is shrouded in gloom. Glory to Thee, my God, for the gladness of little children, for the joy of mothers, for the bliss of lovers. The radiance of their hearts is from Thy touch because in the joy of Thy creation Thou rejoicest. And I praise Thee, my God, that in my unhappiest days there are breaks in the clouds through which I see the blue beyond and the glorious sun of Thy compassionate love. Even a moment of light gives me new hope and new courage to bear the stripes inflicted by my own sins. Praise the Lord. O what great troubles and adversities hast Thou shewed me; yea, and broughtest me from the deeps of the earth again.

The Peace of God

"O let my mouth be filled with thy praise: that I may sing of thy glory and honour all the day long." For Thy forgiveness is abundant and Thy compassion fails not. There is only one pure joy—the union of the soul with God. Praise God that He has not shut this joy from my life but holds it out to me as a fact of the past and a promise for the future. The cloud of my sins is dispersed at the breath of His mouth and the light of His countenance. My scarlet guiltiness becomes white like the driven snow. My mouth praiseth Thee with joyful lips for the past peace, the peace of today, the coming peace that springs from sin forgiven and acceptance in the Beloved.

Songs in the Night

"As for me, I will patiently abide alway: and will praise thee more and more." Even when my heart is heavy and the strings of joy will not vibrate, I can awake the music of praise with my lips. My will to praise perchance may be counted by Thee for praise when the rest of my being is dull and dim and silent. I will patiently wait for Thy reviving breath and will praise Thee more and more with the best member that I have. Give wings to my soul, O my Praise, until it carries my whole being into the heights. My mind adds its power of thought to my will to praise and to rejoice before Thee. My emotions are silent because of my sin. I may not have the comfort of praise but I can and will praise Thee.

The Will

Praised be God for the power of the will. It is Thy power and without Thee it is a menace to myself and my fellows. In its right direction is freedom. By choice we fall: by choice we rise. No choice is free unless it be guided by Thee. No choice is wise except it be inspired by Thy wisdom. I praise Thee, O God, for all the right choices that I have made. I praise Thee for that I can revise all the wrong choices of the past by a new and right choice. Lord, I would praise Thee by choosing right, by choosing Thee instead of me, by choosing Thy way and not mine, by choosing shame and pain if need be rather than honor and ease.

God's Long-suffering

That God has not destroyed me in my sin is all His praise. It is of His mercy that I have not been consumed by His just anger. I merited not only His loving chastisements but the purging of destruction after the flesh. Instead of which Thou hast brought me to honor on every side. Praise God for His long-suffering. He still waits that I may praise Him by living and loving, by self-humiliation to fill the gap which He left through His forbearance. I have never waited for Thee, O God. It is Thou who art always waiting for me. Give me the grace to praise Thee with an obedient will.

Prayer

My Father, were it not for prayer which opens wide the door to Thy heart, where would I be? Blessed be Thy goodness in making it easy for Thy children to approach Thee. Nothing human is too small for Thee to care for. Thy understanding caress soothes every sorrow; Thy wise counsel illumines every problem; Thy limitless pity lightens every burden. So it is, Lord, that with confidence I bring to Thee my prattle. I ask for consolation and Thou givest beyond my asking; I seek for Thy wisdom and I find Thy will for me; I knock at the door of Thy compassion and Thou openest to me Thy treasure of pardon. Praise to Thee, O God, who art ever at our call to renew at our bidding showers of blessing.

Sacraments

The Sacraments are Thyself behind a veil moving into our lives along the path of our Faith. Lord, we would adore Thee for the stubbornness of Thy love which blocks every avenue of escape from Thee. Thou art ever present, even as sunshine and air, giving us of Thy substance without measure and without conscious intake on our part. Thou art ever coming, ever beckoning to us to meet Thee face to face, ever striving to catch our attention by inward appeal and outward symbol. Thou art the untiring servant of the life Thou didst create and endow with Thy likeness. Lord, I would praise Thee by more consecrated use of the sacraments of salvation wherein Thou dost clothe me with love.

Hope

Now, Lord, what is my hope? Truly my hope is even in Thee. Yea, my hope is even Thee. Thou art all promise. In the darkest night Thy star is there to cheer and guide. Hope is power to see a tomorrow containing in it more of good than the today. It is the vision of the end and some purpose of love which makes the lover and the loyal supervictors through Thee who loved us and gave Thyself for us. I thank Thee for the hope of pardon which has over and again saved me from despair in hours of bitter self-reproach and led me where the streams of living, cleansing water flow. I praise Thee for the hope of a better world bound together by unity of spirit in the bond of peace. I praise Thee for the hope that we shall one day clearly see Thy face and share in the fullness of Thy life.

Opportunities

I praise Thee, my Lord God, for my opportunities, the opportunities of yesterday and the opportunities of today. In them I see Thee beckoning with Thy right hand and bidding me enter a door opened into heaven. Thou dost dwell in the midst of opportunity to possess it for us that we may enter in and make it our own. Yesterday I but half seized my inheritance, failing to take it by force, that Kingdom which only yields to force. Today, my God, I would praise Thee for the opportunity that gives me bruised feet and bleeding hands as I move to embrace it. Let my praise declare its measures by my fortitude and patience and loyalty even to the end. Praise the Lord.

Coming Peace

The hope of perfect peace, O Prince of Peace, is most wonderful and precious. Thy peace is to be my peace. It is a tide that is ever rising but which can never be at the full. It wells up within and grows with our growth. The billows of a restless world swell and rage around us but the coming peace is neither stayed nor hindered by their fury. The Kingdom within us where Thy will reigns and is our peace will slowly create the Kingdom without, just as the beautiful Spirit of God breaks out in the dainty bud and the lark's glad song. Lord, I praise Thee for the peace I have and the peace I would have. Peace is not in the hushed stillness of death but in the harmony of ordered life. Lord, give Thy tired world peace, more peace, and still more peace.

Undertake for Me

Lord, undertake for me. Quiet my selfish clamoring. Be Thou my sufficiency. All things happen according to Thy ordering. And if Thou orderest my life, there can be no room for anything but joy when Thy decree goeth forth; for Thy ordering is alone secure. No planning or scheming of mine will mar Thy plan for me. Nothing remains for me but to fit myself into Thy plan. And so shall I reach my highest good and find opportunity for my highest, fullest service. Lord, be Thou my peace. Lay hold of my faculties and train them to Thy use. Inspire me with undying devotion to Thee and Thy will. I am afraid of my weakness. Let it be a vessel to hold Thy strength. Let me not break, O God. Fill me with Divine power.

Sacra Mater

Lord, Thy Bride is my mother. I praise Thee that of her is my spiritual birth. When I was a puling babe she gathered me in her arms and presented me to Thee for safekeeping. All her precious gifts, prayer and song and sacrament, have been mine. At her bosom have I been fed with nourishment to make me strong for conflict and sure for victory. Her arms, restless with love, reach through the great world of men to gather into Thy family and hers those who are far off and nigh. Wounded by her children she never fails to tend and heal the wounded. Broken by angry voices within her family circle she ever counsels peace. Shamed by rents in her beautiful seamless robe she covers her confusion by renewed service. Lord, I praise Thee for Thy Church that is and for Thy Church that is to be.

5. THE GREAT ACT OF WORSHIP

The Eucharist is the Church's great central act of corporate worship. It would be strange, considering the origin of this wonderful mystery, were it otherwise. Even those who regard it as a bare memorial of the historic occurrence of Christ's Passion and nothing more, however highly they may honor the ordinary round of prayer and praise, approach the Eucharist with unwonted awe.

Of course no one conception of its character is complete, as its various and stately names testify. So bound up with the Person of our Lord is it, that, as new treasures of knowledge are laid open concerning Him who is the eternal Son of God, this feast of rich things is proportionately enriched to the participant. Says Jeremy Taylor in his quaint and reverent way: "The Holy Communion or Supper of the Lord is the most sacred, mysterious and useful conjugation of secret and holy things and duties in the religion." And withal it is, in essence, of all simple things the most simple—a meal, a meal transformed and exalted, it is true, but still a meal. However difficult the liturgy may be for unlearned folk, the sacrament itself, "the breaking of the bread," is easily understood by everyone, even the least wise. Nor is it hard to reconcile the idea of a feast with this meager meal of a morsel of bread and a sip of wine; for everyday experience has prepared us for the conveyance of great wealth through what has no intrinsic excellence. If a scrap of paper can have the value of heaps of gold, and, by the law of association, an age-worn trinket can become of priceless worth, it suggests no unreality to claim that under certain conditions a simple meal becomes a royal banquet, filling heart and soul and mind, and admitting into the very presence of the Most Holy and Most High. There is diversity in the explication of this act of worship, but whatever difference of opinion there may be regarding its exact nature, those most widely separated in thought will agree in this, that it is a profound rite, and that in it is spiritual wealth. And in these days, when at last men are beginning to perceive that truth is always greater than its best definition, no one will contend that what he sees in the Eucharist is all that it contains.

The best commentary on the Eucharist is the closing chapter of our Lord's mortal career. The Son of Man, as He approached the Cross, drew nigh to that which throughout His ministry He had viewed as a goal; the crucifixion was what He had been preparing Himself for in all that He said and did throughout His human experience; His whole life was indeed a "long going forth to death." He aspired to reach the moment when He would be lifted up from the earth. He saw and predicted with composure all the horror and shame of the Passion, the betrayal and desertion, the scourging and spitting. But He saw even more clearly the dignity and wonder and majesty of the opportunity contained in it all, and spoke of it with suppressed joy: "I have a baptism to be baptized with; and how am I straitened till it be accomplished!" The Cross would test to the full His obedience to God and reveal to what lengths Divine love would go to redeem sinful man. When men near the goal of their innocent ambition their cup of joy is full; nor was Christ's less than full. In the first Eucharist the pain of self-sacrifice for the time being was lost in the joy of self-fulfillment. When He took the bread and the wine and said, "This is My Body which is broken for you," "This is My Blood which is shed for you," He made the sacrifice of Himself. It is this act which separates His death from all other deaths, transforming the crucifixion from a judicial murder into a triumph of self-oblation. It is not the Cross which explains the Eucharist, but rather the Eucharist which explains the Cross. Eliminate the Eucharist from the story of the Passion and our Lord's death sinks from the atoning act by which the world is reconciled to God into a mere act of resignation to a painful fate, to be classed with the death of Socrates and like heroes. It is the Eucharist that enables us to say that the crucifixion was a sacrifice; that however true it is that Christ was put to death by sinful men, it is a truth of greater magnitude that, according to His repeated prediction, He laid down His life for His friends; that the Cross of Calvary, and through it every cross that bows the shoulders of men, has become the instrument of victory and a school of obedience and sympathy.

No act of Christ was a mere personal experience. The Son of Man, as in loving sympathy He declared Himself to be, was the Universal Character whose life must needs concern and touch all other lives. It was His expressed desire that His fellows should share all that He was and did. He, the Son of God, became the Son of Man that we might become Sons of God. Therefore it is not surprising that, at this the supreme moment of His life, He should bid the representative group who companied with Him, and through them all men, come in and participate in its power and joy; He did not merely lay down His life, but asked others to enter into His experience, saying, "Take, eat; this is My Body." "Drink ye all of this; this is My Blood." For what is the import of this invitation but this? "Associate yourselves with Me—aye, be one with Me, incorporated into Me, in this great moment of self-offering; for I would present you a willing surrender in and with Myself." The idea of at-one-ment was never more intelligible than in these latter days. We are becoming more and more conscious of how close-wrought are the fibers of the human race; we recognize how the life of any one man affects the life of his fellows, and how the individual can gather into his own soul the sorrows and joys, the perplexities and aspirations of many

people. If this is part of the experience of *a* son of man, it
follows that *the* Son of Man, by the extension and completion
of that quality which, when found in us, is known as sympathy,
if by nothing else beyond—and the character of His personality
tells us there is much beyond that is inexplicable—not only
may but must take into Himself and hold there for time and
eternity the whole race—except so far, alas, as men struggle
from the freedom of His embrace into the slavery of a false
independence. Thus the Eucharist is the divinely chosen
means whereby we men are invited to enter into, and con-
sciously to appropriate the highest points of the victory of the
Cross as well as what lies beyond—the resurrection life.
Through it He shares with us His life-giving death and His
deathless life, His Divine nature and His perfect humanity,
and we are "accepted in the Beloved."

The various titles of the sacrament of Christ's Body and
Blood suggest its various aspects, one of which, and that the
one that happily is most common in our Church, we shall
consider—the Holy Communion. This title indicates the view
of the sacrament which most readily appeals to the human
heart. The Holy Communion means, of course, "the Holy
Fellowship"—not "a" but "the," that fellowship which above
all others is holy, the end of which is to make all who participate in it holy. It is fellowship with the Father in Christ—
not merely with Christ, the Son of God and the Son of Man as
He is, is the "Way" to the Father. Nor is it an ordinary fellowship, of which the fellowship of mere men is a complete
image. Ordinary fellowship allows two lives to intertwine; but
here so close is the relationship that "Christ *with* us," "we *with*
Christ" is inadequate to describe the intimacy, and "we *in*
Christ," "Christ *in* us," phrases which no one dare to apply

to any other friendship, can alone tell the tale. And "we in Christ" not "Christ in us" is the grander and more frequent phrase. "In Christ" tells of the unmeasured wealth of fellowship, divine and human, which is the Christian heritage; it is the whole parable of the vine and the branches in two syllables. This is the Godward aspect of the sacrament. And in this connection three things are to be noted:

1. Every fresh communion is a new point of contact with God in Christ through the working of the Eternal Spirit; each last communion means more than any of those which have gone before, as even in our association with a human friend new qualities and untried depths of familiar characteristics are revealed in each successive act of intercourse. Friendship is taken up day by day on a higher level than formerly, because of these new glimpses of the inner recesses of life which are caught from time to time as friends meet. And frequent repetition of the sacrament ought no more to impair its value, than frequent meetings the reality of friendship.

2. Communion is only begun and not ended at the altar. It is something more than a touch for a moment. Grace is not the infusion of some mysterious spiritual property, which God having imparted leaves the recipient to make use of by himself; grace is the gift of God's personal working in the life through the indwelling Spirit. God never holds His faithful children one moment to let them go the next. He enfolds us in Himself with a tightening embrace, as by loyalty to His laws and repeated acts of faith, we expose new portions of our nature for Him to lay hold on. The sense of God's presence may be peculiarly full as we kneel to receive the heavenly food, just as at the moment of meeting again one whom we love the emotions are deeply stirred; but by virtue of yesterday's commun-

ion, God is as near at hand today as He was when we received
the sacrament. The Holy Communion would fail in its purpose
if it made the presence of our Lord a reality only for the time
being, and did not more fully introduce men into the Divine
presence as an abiding state. The fact of God's immanence in
us requires this conclusion.

3. The result of a faithful reception of the Holy Communion
should be holiness in the common, everyday life, from which
an incident, the family meal, is borrowed and transformed as
the symbol and means by which all other incidents may be
transformed. So great a mystery demands all the majesty of a
liturgy and the accompaniment of stately worship; and a
dignified ritual attached to this representative, this common
act of our human life, is most valuable as indicating the majesty of all that is commonplace when it is touched by God. Just
as we consecrate certain times and seasons in order that all
times and seasons may become holy, so in the sacraments God
has taught us to consecrate the simplest acts of ordinary life—
the bath and the meal—as typical of the potential sacredness
of all acts, and as a means of sanctifying and ennobling them.
So the Holy Communion touches alike private life and life in
society, the life of recreation and the life of business, and unless
it transfigures each of these departments of human experience
it falls short of its purpose. Let the businessman remember
that he strains to see and touch the Most Holy at the altar
that he may see and touch the Most Holy in the market; let
the professional man and the man of letters, the day laborer
and the scientist each in his sphere be carried from the vision
of God in the Eucharist to the abiding fellowship with God
in his special vocation. He who comes *from* God goes *to* God,
whithersoever his steps may bear him. The presence of our

Lord at the altar is special but not exclusive. It is not a lamp lighted for a moment and then put out, but a light which will illuminate all life, and enable us to see at every turn the vision of omnipresent Love. It is one function of the sacraments to enhance, not to dim, the reality of God's immanence in all His works; to train us to perceive and apprehend that

> Earth's crammed with heaven
> And every common bush afire with God,—

a declaration which otherwise would be held to be but a poet's fickle fancy or a vague philosophical idea. Days are coming, if they are not already upon us, when in the midst of scientific progress and explanation in which men are prone to rest as final, the believer's ceaseless theme must be the Divine in-dwelling. And the strongest and most telling means of keeping alive this truth for ourselves and others is the sacramental system of the Church.

Thus far we have been thinking of the Godward aspect of the Holy Communion—fellowship with God in Christ. On its manward side it is fellowship with man in Christ. As it sustains us in Divine fellowship and lifts us continually into purer heights, so it assures us of our incorporation in the mystical Body of Christ, "which is the blessed company of all faithful people," and inspires us to deeper love. Here again it is necessary to recall the original simple form of the sacrament, a form so simple that, as Bishop Westcott says somewhere, it is difficult in the earliest references to it to distinguish it from the ordinary family meal. The brethren gather around the com-mon table and partake of the common loaf. And the use of the one loving-cup from which all drink goes beyond the customs of ordinary family life. The Holy Communion, which is a social act, speaks of the transformation of social life. Just as the constant sharing of food at one table is the pledge of loyal service to one another on the part of all who partake, as well as a means of gaining strength to fulfill the pledge, so the Holy Communion is a pledge to mutual service and equipment for its accomplishment. "In Christ" a new relationship is established between man and man, or rather an old relationship is deepened and consummated. Brethren after the flesh are made brethren in the Lord. Family and national ties are very sacred and very close, but they reach the full purpose which God designed for them only when they become the basis for spiritual kinship. It is considered a dreadful thing, and rightly so, when men of common blood are at variance with one another; nothing is more shameful than a family feud. And on the other hand, blood relationship is in itself a demand for the most loyal service that men are capable of rendering. Now through the sacramental life a kinship is established and sustained as real and as binding as that consequent upon the accident of birth; so that for Christian to be at variance with Christian is as unnatural as it is for two of one family to strive with one another; for Christian to overreach Christian is as treacherous as it was for Jacob to steal Esau's blessing. The loyalty which those who are "in Christ" owe one another is the loyalty due among those who sit at the same board and eat of the same loaf, among those in whose veins runs the blood of a common mother. When men learn the reality and force of spiritual kinship, social problems will be solved and social evils will cease.

But a hasty glance has been bestowed in the foregoing pages on a mystery of unsearchable depth, and many of its aspects have not even been noted. The more obvious aspects are the ones upon which stress has been laid as including in them all others. As with all other forms of approach to God, so here, what a man knows about the Holy Communion is that which God has taught him in his reception of the Sacrament. Those who would fain plumb its depths must come frequently and preparedly to the feast. Nor is preparation a formal act. It is unfortunate that some teachers make it so by laying insistence on a set form. The best, and indeed the only, true preparation is an outcome of a full knowledge of the thing for which we wish to prepare ourselves, just as the best thanksgiving for a blessing is the spontaneous utterance consequent upon a contemplation of the gift received. The man who knows the spiritual significance of the Holy Communion, *ipso facto* knows how to prepare to receive it.

· 4 ·

The Last Great Adventure

1. PRESENCE: HUMAN AND DIVINE

It is an illustrative sort of definition that I shall attempt of Presence. Presence is the operative result of relationships of whatever sort. It is juxtaposition and all that contact or interpenetration involves. That which constitutes presence is stated for me in the words of a modern philosopher: "A body is present wherever its (attractive) influence is felt."[1] Such a definition implies degrees of presence to an infinite extent, varying from an indestructible union to an attraction of such slender tenuity as to be only just more than zero. With this in mind it is proper further to aver that "When we observe that a thing really *is* there where it *acts*, we shall be led to say that all the atoms interpenetrate and that each of them fills the world."[2] It is important to maintain this to be so, for if we were to restrict presence to mere physical contiguity, unity would be a mirage, or at best a bundle of faggots, instead of that balancing and relationship of the sum total of forces which

[1] Bergson's *Creative Evolution*, p. 198.
[2] *Ibid.*, p. 214.

makes us neighbors with the farthest fixed star as securely as with the threshold of our home.

Man is fully present to man only so far as there is mutual and volitional give and take. Presence is due to self-expression in general or special terms, or both. This is given or withheld at will. A man may be nearer the farthest star than his nearest neighbor. The star through the spectroscope yields up the secrets of its inmost being, whereas the man robes himself in inscrutability. This reaches its summit in antagonism, that is, in absence. Who could have been more completely absent than at the end was Christ in the presence of Pilate? Pilate had not the power, or refused to use the power, to recognize Christ. Christ reached after every possible point of contact afforded by Pilate's character and attitude until the last avenue was closed.

Hence human presence not only has its degrees, but its volitional degrees. A man is as little, or as much, present as he chooses. He can give or withhold. In the case of Christ and Pilate, though Pilate was present to Christ, Christ was not always or fully present to Pilate. Christ read Pilate through and through. He needed not that anyone should bear witness concerning man; for He Himself knew what was in man. On the other hand sordid motives bound Pilate's eyes so that he could not see Christ. Jesus gave him no answer. He was absent.

It is always the case when a man pretends to be what he is not, or when from selfish motives, he makes an effort to create a distinguished impression of himself on others, it is a false impression. He creates not a relationship between himself and his fellows, but rather builds a barrier preventing such relationship. He enunciates an absence.

Volitional presence has unique power. A man may offer his presence to a fellow without gaining response. The other man may refuse self-expression and meet advances with repudiation and hatred. But the friend may to a certain extent compel the other's presence. He may seize upon and hold wise fellowship with the best of his foe. "I would be friend to all—the foe—the friendless," that is a triumph of human presence. "Love them that hate you," is not a sentimental rhapsody, but a calm recognition of the fact, that volitional presence can both press itself successfully on one refusing to receive it, and seize upon the presence of one refusing to give it. It is this which forms the most thrilling part of our whole wonderful life of adventure and struggle.

Love is, in its supreme triumphs, volitional rather than emotional. It creates affinities out of antagonisms, presences out of absences, friends out of enemies. Herein it displays its magic power, and finds its secret rejoicings. Its zest is for men rather than for selected men. Its method is to draw out the richest presence by offering the richest presence. Its law is devotion to persons, beginning with God and ending with man, the last and the least. Its domain, therefore, is everywhere, all the time. Love, and consequently human presence, cannot be expressed in terms of time or space. Nothing can loosen the grasp of love on a presence which it wills to retain. To attempt to do so is only to tighten its hold.

Friendship consists in mutual and constant volitional presence. Physical contacts are eternized between friends. But they are not permanently essential. We have a high degree of sensitiveness that is extra spatial and extra temporal. Friendship, though fostered by, is not dependent upon, automatic or sensory presence. Often it is deepened and eternized best by physical absence. Christ enunciated a truth of wide application and bearing when he said to His friends, "It is expedient for you that I go away. If I go not away the Comforter will not come unto you. If I go away I will send Him unto you."

Human presence is so completely volitional that distance is no bar to its operation. My friends, whether in the uttermost parts of the Earth or in Paradise, are with me when I will them so to be, and up to a certain point, in the degree I will them to be. Time is as little a barrier as space. Plato, Francis of Assisi or Lincoln comes at my bidding or beckoning. It is more than an act of memory that brings them, though that noble faculty has its share not merely in recalling but restoring and transfiguring past relationships. When there is developed sensitiveness there is no knowing how conscious such fellowship or presence may become. The wireless telephone may be a sign of a future possible correspondence between soul and soul where space or time interpose to check fellowship. This is speculative, but authenticated psychic experience in numerous cases tends to encourage belief in it.

In dreams souls, widely separated, often touch and mingle. Sleep among other things is the will's relaxation or holiday. It is the suspension of volitional and conscious contacts. The will is the most unremitting of human faculties. It is the controlling force of life, and when quiescent it gives the rest of the human make-up its opportunity for repose. There are times when the affections, the imagination, the reasoning powers, wake up before the will. So, unrestrained, they dart to their nearest affinity—the affections to the most available friend, the intellect to its most absorbing task, the imagination to the nearest garden. The awakened faculties are, without the active leadership of the will, like a child wandering about the countryside without a guardian, and often they lose themselves in the labyrinths of the grotesque and ill-proportioned. This is the stuff that dreams are made of.

Death sets powers free so that presence may be extended. This is not a speculative assertion but a fact of history capped by the common experience of men of today. The idealization of those who have gone is simply their self-realization as viewed from our side. The incidental faults of weakness, the contra-volitional self, drops out of sight and we see the character in its main features. It is a pity that the living are not judged by their contemporaries with the same lofty effort to be fair that characterizes our judgment of the dead. Though a man's character is declared in his actions, frequently the moral color of an action is to be determined by his character, rather than vice versa.

The greater a man is the greater his power of presence. A world-hero like the Buddha, or Livingstone, is one whose presence is universally available—not as an echo or an influence but as a person, not as one who lived but as one who lives. How conscious this output of presence is to the person from whom it flows, how much due to present propulsion, I cannot say. But anyone who has eternized his mortality no longer belongs to time but has become an eternal force. He practices eternity. He has gone beyond the Aristotelian injunction which of late it has become popular to quote: "Wherefore, in so far as we can, we must practice immortality, and do our utmost to live according to the highest principle within us." The immortality of influence perpetuated in time is real though limited. But it is always personal pressure that tells. True character not only refuses to die at the bidding of death, but stands forth with new and compelling power at the very moment when the logic of space and time argue vehemently for its cessation. The eternal cannot die, because by the law of its being it is not subject to death: it is indifferent to it where it does not use it to its own advantage. What we call immortal is that aspect of the eternal which finds expression in volitional presence. After death an eternized personality lives as spirit, personal spirit, unobscured by the veil of the flesh. The presence not only abides, but continues to operate, here in a refined manner. It is not that it alters its mode of operation, but that we who remain perceive that which hitherto was only partially apparent to us. We often attribute influence to the incidentals of personality instead of to the eternized personality which death unveils. So far as it affects persons and builds them up it is because it is personal. The sole upbuilder of personality is personality. Things are incapable of making human character, and so are ideas, except to the extent that they are personified or recognized as being controlled and directed by personality.

The question of volitional malevolent presence could be discussed in terms similar to those used for the consideration of volitional benevolent presence. With the exception of a single thought in this connection I shall not dwell upon it. This must be remembered, however, it is only like that can be present to like. Enmity is absence. Light has no fellowship with darkness. It can have none. Hence a malevolent presence cannot force itself upon us so as to pollute us, so as really to touch our life, unless we ourselves will evil. It may make an appeal to us for entrance into our audience chamber where fellowship is alone possible, but that is only to tempt us. As long as our volitional presence is withheld all is well. A degree of aloofness is reached by repeated acts of volitional absence in the face of an appeal for fellowship on the part of evil, that makes the evil nonexistent so far as we are concerned. It no longer has power even to tempt us. There must be evil in us volitionally responding to that which assails us, before evil is present to us as a deterrent force. As long and as often as we meet it by volitional absence it fails to find foothold in our world and becomes for us decreasingly a reality. When it speaks we answer not a word.

Man is always volitionally present to God. God is omnipresent in the sense of always holding all men in His consciousness. God is always automatically or unconsciously or subconsciously present to man. Religion is the making of the automatic volitional, the unconscious conscious, the sensory spiritual, the physical symbolic.

God's presence among men was focused by Christ. In a sense Christ created God's presence among men. He made it available. God was manifested, that is made present, in Him. It is fitting at this point reverently to conjecture, that one reason why God chose man through whom to make his highest revelation was because man is, of all creation, the most intelligible, the most present, object to man. Humanity is more present to us than animals of the lower sort or than things. Human life is the only thing we know from a constant and inside experience. Moreover it is the most worthy, as well as the least unintelligible, of things created. Every attempt of religion to apprehend God through animals and things, as the final symbol has ended in idolatry or the substitution of darkness for light, the symbol for that symbolized. When things or ideas rather than persons are given first place, or too high attention, in the processes of religion, God becomes obscured, because the less rather than the more intelligible is chosen as the medium of approach.

As a historic figure Christ has a presence of the same sort as, though in a higher degree than, every other great personality. His presence is that of Plato and the Buddha, the difference being that theirs is in an imperfect, and His in the supreme, degree. His character and relationships were complete, therefore His presence is universal. His volitional presence was laid at the feet of mankind for their acceptance. Herein is love not that we loved Him but that He first loved us. He willed to be and eternally is the Light of the World, the Bread of Life, the Way, the Truth and the Life. In His mortality He was such a Personality as men had hitherto only dimly conceived of.

But Christ is no bare historic figure. His presence is not due to mere unconscious immortality. God's eternity rests at the heart of Christ's immortality. "Lo I am with you always even unto the ages of ages," is the necessary result of His being who He is. The universal Person must offer a universal presence, human and Divine, the Divine through the human.

When the mortality of Christ was finally conquered, He delocalized His presence, not to decrease, but on the contrary to intensify it, to make possible a new and inclusive localization. The Christ spirit represents not a lesser but a greater, not a contracted but an expanded, self-personification or personalization. The more spiritual a personality becomes, the more intensely real it grows to be, and so the more widely and deeply available. His presence becomes an atmosphere and influence without losing its transcendent completeness in the luxuriance of its increased immanence. The presence of the Paraclete took the place of the localized Christ not as a bare substitute but as that which constitutes a superior presence, including all that it held formerly and adding greatness to greatness, riches to wealth. In going, Christ came in a fullness which was wanting before He went, the fullness of added availability, a higher degree of presence. But just as before, His presence is all willed and graded. It is the presence of a Person. He is present under specified conditions for declared purposes, whether in the midst of two or three gathered in His name, or in the pure waters of Baptism and the simple feast of Communion (i.e., fellowship or presence). He encourages representative acts of localization, that in finding Him here and there we may have practice so as to be able to find Him everywhere. The most wonderful localizing of God is implied in the saying of Christ that "the Kingdom of God is within you." It is one whether we locate God here in the sacrament, or there beyond space—near or far it is localizing Him. To say that He is immanent, filling His creation, is localizing Him quite as much as to postulate His presence at any point in His creation. If my limitations as man (or, maybe, it is my glorious liberty as God's child) require me to localize Him in order to make real His presence, I prefer localizing Him in a sacrament of His institution, rather than in a flower of His handiwork. The flower is the product of His first creative work; the sacrament is the product of His second creative work—creation playing upon creation. The sin of localizing, when it is a sin, consists not in localizing, but in exclusive localizing—here, and not there, instead of there because here, here for this purpose, there for that purpose, transcendent because immanent, immanent because transcendent, immanent and transcendent because a Person.

Symbols of God as revealed in Christ must always connote God's presence in a high degree. To preserve or use a symbol of God in any way short of the sacramental would be to empty it of its meaning, and create a religious distraction instead of a religious aid. So far as church sacraments are an aid to the intensification of the Christ-spirit presence, it is because of a recognition of representative localization and immediacy, not of an act of stimulated memory, groping through a remote century, in a search for a Christ that once was, a presence of yesterday. Carrying logic to its pitiless conclusion, a religious symbol which is not a symbol of Our Lord's presence is a symbol of His absence, and therefore abhorrent formalism. To say that Christ instituted a sacrament is tantamount to saying that He representatively localized Himself, in the chosen token for specified purposes and under stated conditions.

In His intensification of relationships, Christ changed "with" to "in"—the spirit of truth "abideth with you and shall be in you." Presence finds its completion in interpenetration—"abide in me and I in you." There is nothing beyond this. Life in Christ is sufficient for here and there. Hope can discover nothing higher. The Beatific Vision, theology's best attempt to express the *summum bonum* of life, is presence that is at once constant and ecstatic. God is all in all.

2. TRUST IS THE VICTORY

It is our duty to look at the unfearful side of death. Let it be said, with the glorious certainty that belongs to the assertion, death in its Christian character is a superb victory, crowning all the victories of life.

The terror of death is in ourselves rather than in death. Christ made clear by illustration that in Him death was a new upward and onward stride. Apart from life as a Son of God it is animal dissolution. As the last experience, like birth a sort of boundary experience, of the life of a Son of God it is spiritual transfiguration.

I believe that it is the horror and fear of dying that is our chief trouble. The protracted suffering, the fading faculties, the repulsiveness of the natural processes, lead us astray. Probably all of us would choose, if we were allowed to, the manner of our going. We would prefer to stride out quickly at an opportune moment. We would avoid the autumnal method for ourselves and others. But the autumn, the canker and the storm are for men as for trees. Whatever the guise in which death greets us, death is in itself never more and never less than death.

The moment is an opportune one in which to get a truer and more wholesome and more whole view of death than that which ordinarily prevails. There is too much black about Christian death. If for us it is a hard discipline to say good-bye for a while, the going from earth marks a gala day for the one who goes. The house of death should abjure the artificial. The tone of triumph should dominate our farewell. We cannot force ourselves into this temper of mind, but it will follow on as the logical result of a Christian view of death.

We can afford to leave the time and the manner of death to Him Who is the Conqueror of death. We should shut our minds to a consideration of these elements over which we have no control.

The first and best illustration of the effect upon personality of death is found in Jesus Christ. After His reappearance from the grave He is unaltered in character, tone of thought and fundamental relationships. He is the Son of Man that He was, with widened scope and powers, and freedom from, in the best sense of the word, unnaturalness. The life of His companions fits into His and His into theirs. What strikes one forcibly is the absence of anything like a break in the continuity of His personality.

If we think of death as an introduction into conditions wholly foreign and unsuited to human nature, death must be something to be feared. It is unwonted in that it is untried. But it is thoroughly human in that it is part of universal human experience. It is suited to us. It is the next thing we need when we have finished here. Our Lord promises by His own representative career what will happen to us.

The reality of the world to come! In this past year bitter partings and unlooked-for sorrows have entered into our lives. Friends have gone into new and distant fields of labor; we have been bereaved as individuals, as a parish, as a nation; and we ought to dwell much on the reality of the world to come. It is only when that other world becomes more real than this that we can face bereavement not simply with fortitude, but with bounding hope. Christ speaks of Paradise with firm assurance; and of going thither as though it might be to Jerusalem or Capernaum. He has been thinking much about it, and when He speaks of it to His new-found follower His tones carry conviction so that he too rejoices in anticipation of the beautiful land yonder where he is to be with the King. The penitent robber thinks crudely no doubt of that new country. To him it is a place of physical delight where the wind blows through stately palms, and glad rivers race to the sea over fertile plains. But it is real, a land near by. He and his

Companion, Christ, are but a step away, for they are to enter it *today*.

Our realization of that land at best must be crude. But do not let us be afraid of talking of Paradise and Heaven as *places*. Doubtless they are *conditions*. But the common mind does not grasp what is baldly transcendental. We must be more or less anthropomorphic, we must project our ideas of life as we know it beyond the grave. Nor is there any reason to be ashamed of so doing. Christ chose a term, "Paradise," suited to the comprehension of the man He was dealing with. He gave him something concrete, real. The metaphysician might find occasion to cavil at the materialism lurking behind the word. But Christ used it because it had substance for the ex-robber, it was something upon which he could exercise a living faith. Look up then to that real land where in quiet joy dwell your loved ones who have gone before.

Its chief characteristic is joyousness. Paradise is a glad word, fragrant with delight. Call it Purgatory if you will, if by Purgatory you mean a place where the last traces of sin are done away by the boundless tenderness of God. But the souls at rest are happy suffering souls; our earliest experience there will be to feel the caress of God. Paradise is not a prison house of torture; it is a palace of joy. The name tells of the Garden of God where He is the sufficient Food, and where the redeemed, transfigured, move from strength to strength in endless progress toward perfection; a garden where there is fellowship—"with Me"; where "angel faces smile which we have loved long since and lost awhile."

And God wishes Paradise to begin now inasmuch as He invites us to be with Him now. Soon, sooner than we dream of perhaps, we shall be bidden to move out and up through the

gate of death to join the souls at rest. There we shall wait for
the final triumph. God speed the day when the joys of Paradise
shall rise to the still greater completeness of Heaven! for

> . . . lo! there breaks a yet more glorious day;
> The Saints triumphant rise in bright array;
> The King of Glory passes on His way.
> Alleluia!

How shall we be able to trust God in great things, if we have
never had enough faith to trust Him in small things? How
shall we have any confidence at the hour of death in One whose
love and power we have never allowed ourselves to experience
in life? Our money, our genius, our luck, our ideas, our plans,
carried us through life. God was not in our thoughts. Believe
me, there will come a day when "the cord is frayed and the
cruse is dry." There will be nothing left for us to do but trust;
and what if we find ourselves without the capacity of faith?
The shadows of death will try the temper of our life, of what
sort it is—our motives, our ambitions, our belief in God's personal providence. As far as we are concerned the foundations
of the firmament will be broken up. Then will it be made
evident to whom we have given the glory, whether to God or
to self. No self-confidence can carry us through death—nothing but the power of God evoked by trust on our part.

Today is the hour in which to learn the lesson of trust. What
comfort to know that the life which was lived wholly in the
atmosphere of trust was the only complete life in human
history! What gladness and encouragement in the assurance
that God has never once failed, not merely to respond to trust,
but to surprise trust by giving beyond its fairest expectations!
What peace to live in the knowledge that we need not worry

about the terrors of death as we look ahead and anticipate our last hour; if we but trust now we shall be able to trust with a practiced faith then, as Christ trusted, and there will be "light at evening time." Christ, who in Himself conquered death, will repeat His victory in us and for us.

Thus it is that in the Cross we find our sufficient consolation. Our faltering hearts grow brave as we contemplate Jesus of the Passion. What larger consolations can life hold than those revealed in the royal bequest of the Saviour's dying words? Here they are once more, compressed into brief compass: The largest hope is not denied the worst; forgiveness is not merely a remission, but an admission—yes, more than an admission, a commission, to fellowship with God in Christ; the home and the nation together with the Church form God's triple throne on earth; Christ endured to the limit, even to taking upon Him the sins of the world; He went through the abyss of pain that it might become to us the ladder of achievement; in duty done is exultant joy, even when suffering is at its height; trust is victory, whether in life or in death.

3. TO FRIENDS IN BEREAVEMENT

I have the quiet consolation, steadily growing, that death is only an incident, and that its power has been so broken that it can do little else than create a momentary break in inter-communication. Love somehow becomes more of a steady flame through death. If we hold in our inmost hearts those who have gone, and they in like manner hold us, death is already abolished.

I have just passed anniversaries of deaths in our family— mother, brother, sister, and shortly another brother—each year brighter and gladder festivals. My relationship with those who have gone before is not a relationship with figures of the past, but with living, loving comrades, "mystic sweet communion with those whose rest is won." It is easy to let it become a mere matter of memory. Memory has, of course, its part to play. I have tried to remember my mother's voice, its tones or music, her look, her manner, as so many treasures. But that is not enough. In itself it tends to bring grief over loss and a sense of emptiness. Our relationship instead is a reality of now from moment to moment. You here and the loved one there are united in a common love, a common purpose and a common work. It is a transference of fellowship from the seen to the unseen, a deepening, not a lessening of ties, communion rather than communication. It is of the same order as our mystic tie with God. It could not be less or otherwise. Memory goes back to mortality, faith rises into the uplands of the eternal and the super-real. I have often pondered those words of our Lord to His loved companions—"It is good for you that I go away." The perfection of fellowship cannot be consummated until it becomes all real, remembering the mystical is the real. You and I, by the very withdrawal of our dear ones, get to know them better than we could ever know them under conditions of mortality.

It is a fact of history that the greatest figures are not known until after they die—from Socrates to Christ, and from Christ to Lincoln. What is true of the greater is true of the lesser. When Bishop Westcott, great scholar and great character, lost his wife, his friends noticed a kind of grave gladness that seemed to possess him. I covet the same for you. It is quite one thing to be exalted for a bit, carried by emotion, which must have its reaction. That means harsh suppression of natural (and spiritual) instincts which always carries its penalties. It is another matter to keep one's inner life quietly and steadily on a high mystic plane where peace loves to dwell and where you can operate even under the clouds of sorrow. So we will look upward, not back. We shall continue to hold fellowship with a living person and not with a mere memory.

It is good in praying for the beloved dead to let our minds soar a bit, so that we shall think of them in their new and expanded life very much as we would were they across the seas, only with unclouded confidence for we know that they are free from all alarms and are joyous and strong. Tennyson's "In Memoriam" has often been to me fascinating with its sad, wondering solace. Its lack is largely in its failure to bring out the "mystic sweet communion." The poet's wings of faith droop even when his imagination is at its best.

The mystery of the tragic is largely solved by the young man Jesus, who mounted the cross at an age when it is hardest to die. More than that, His death became His chiefest asset of service and the supreme joy of His deathless life. By that way which God knows so well your grief eventually will be transformed into your chief glory. The days that lie immediately ahead will open up to you with all sorts of unexpected aids and inspirations and encouragements. Your nature, born for Christian service, turned to Christian service, is going to be enriched and empowered in a way that more than ever will make you a leader and guide for others.

I always try to follow a redeemed soul into the life beyond. With his blameless life, his lofty purpose, and his simple faith, he is already at home in the great society of Christ. His love for you is all that it has ever been and will remain unchanged until you meet again—and in the meantime there is the unbreakable mystic bond that defies all forces that would separate.

There is a "mystic sweet communion with those whose rest is won." I try to think of them as they are now—alive with such life as hitherto they have never known, pulsating with that love for you which you know so well, rejoicing in reunion with those dear to them. In the midst of blinding tears one can say these things with profound conviction that they are true. Grief is inconsolable in that the gap made can never be filled with anyone else than the beloved. I stand near enough to the grave to know the cruelty of the gulf that separates, but the realization of it does not weaken faith.

Some people resent the thought that time is a healer. None the less it is. Time decorates and transfigures sorrows until beauty shines through the wound and comfort swallows the grief. Then, too, in the case of bereavement, time carries us with steady and sure stream toward that reunion which is the complete compensation for the temporary separation from those "loved long since and lost awhile." The desire to hear the voice and feel the touch of a vanished loved one must be keen. It but bears witness to the intensity of our love. But, after all, what is a voice or a hypothetical voice which speaks in foreign tones and which is separated by an unbridgeable gulf from the total personality? A voice without the personality behind it, hearing through a medium without sight and sense to me is utterly empty. So it is that spiritism to me is devoid of attraction and beauty and reality. Nor do I know a single instance where its effort has worked for good and not for evil.

Love must live on memory, mystic communion (not communication), and hope, if it is to do its full work.

It may be that it is because I have gone far on life's journey and am rapidly nearing the end that time seems to me a small matter and that I do not grow impatient. Yet it has been always so, more or less. It is the certainty of the goal which steadies me. There is nothing more sure than that in the multitude which no man could number toward which we are whirling no one will be lost in the crowd. No one can be mistaken for another, so individual is each of the human beings that "has breathed this human breath." The question of baby, child and full-grown man is not decisive. It is love that unites; not intellect, which divides. On the basis of the child-like character the Kingdom of Heaven is reared and although there is growth in the Beyond, it is growth toward, not from, those of us who remain. For the Kingdom of Heaven is composed only of little children or those who, growing old, retain or regain their childhood.

I think it takes a long experience and much personal suffering before one begins to understand the satisfaction—I can think of no other word—to the mourner of the pain of bereavement. How often we hear someone say, "Ten years ago my mother died, and I have never been reconciled to her loss." It is a comfort of comforts to know that nothing can quench the yearning for the beloved less than the personal presence and touch of the beloved himself. This is love's testimony to its own reality and depth. We would not have it otherwise. The beating pain becomes a half joy. Side by side with this is the mystic triumph, in that the stream of love from the beloved to us is as full, as steady, as that from us to the beloved, the real unity of life has not so much as been broken, to say nothing of having ceased. As the new relationship (wholly mystical as it now is) settles into the chief part of life, analogous to our mystical union with Christ, our loneliness is relieved by its silent power and in some measure ceases.

Our thoughts and work are shared thoughts and work. We think and do with and for the beloved in his mystic presence just as we did in his bodily presence. It is thus that sorrow and pain become a source of power, quickening to service and giving point to action.

Another towering fact is that mortality is our Kindergarten experience, our earliest conscious knowledge of a life that is not only everlasting but, more mysterious and wonderful still, also eternal. Space and time are seeming tyrants but neither is to be feared for our immortality smiles at both as we begin to practice it here and await with reverent curiosity for the wonders that are hidden behind successive veils of experience of which death is the last. Of course no one can help the suffering which comes in bereavement. Indeed who would escape it if he could? It is the one means left to us by which to declare the reality and depth of our love for the one taken. Were there no pain it would mean there had been no love or little love. Go on unanxiously with the glad knowledge that you and yours are tied by a bond against which death is as powerless as is a cloud to extinguish the sun or a hammer to destroy a moonbeam.

In these later years I have come to view life as being in itself tragedy. There is no escape. If it does not come in one form it does in another. What then? Here Christ and Chris-

tianity come in—not as a consolation merely when we share
the common lot, but as an armor and a transforming power
which make us victorious in defeat and in all things super-
conquerors. Love is invincible, whether it be God's love for us,
or ours for Him or for one another. The companionship you
and your husband had through the happy years of your mar-
ried life is still yours and will be a thing of joy forever. Neither
his love for you nor yours for him has been weakened, much
less destroyed, by death. On the contrary it has been intensified. The face to face comradeship may be suspended for a
time. In the meanwhile it is for us who remain to prepare
ourselves to be at our best when the moment of reunion comes.

As one grows in experience the tragic character of life becomes more and more evident. On the other hand the brave
and often glad way in which people meet their troubles is a
witness to the triumph over tragedy which makes life worth
while. It is of no special value for us to speculate as to why
these things must be. The world is what it is by God's appointment and our business is to feel for His hand "among all the
changes and chances of this mortal life." It is a hand of love.
Out of all the dimness and pain will be born an "eternal
weight of glory." I do not know what "glory" means but it
does suggest that complete satisfaction and victory for which
the human heart longs. In the meantime we must play our
part, not by lapsing into self-pity or succumbing to depression,
but by showing ourselves strong in the strength of Christ who
went through the most extreme suffering with tranquillity.
After all, it is not death that is so dreadful. It is the painful
and tragic avenue to death from which one shrinks. The consolation remains that God is true and will not leave any hard

experience without ultimate and surprising compensation. We are still "prisoners of hope."

As I have moved on in years I have reached a stable and tried philosophy of life which I think is Christian and, so far as I am concerned, invigorating in every conceivable vicissitude. The first grim fact frankly to admit without reservations or self-deceit is that this mortal life is tragedy. The next thing is to discover how to deal with it. Christ in supreme tragedy has declared by a classic instance that the worst cannot injure or destroy anything of real value or importance. Personality is superior to the worst shock of evil, provided personality is allied to God in Christ. Love is not only unharmed and undimmed by sorrow, shame, pain, and death but rises out of it burnished, beautified, and more than triumphant. Masefield's great poem "Good Friday" brings this out as no other literary masterpiece with which I am familiar save Holy Writ. The blind beggar becomes a replica in his sphere of the victor of the Cross. Our worst, in the last analysis our only, enemy is fear, and "perfect love casteth out all fear." But there is something beyond that still. Tragedy professes to be the destroyer of peace and joy. Whereas the true believer in God discovers that peace and joy of the enduring sort are born in turbulence and suffering. In one sense life is a game. We make our adventure boldly and if outer defeat is our portion—well, "my own courage, that they did not take." To me the one nightmare is guilt or the fear of guilt. Even then the forgiveness of God is so complete that He shows us how to make capital out of our worst sorrow and blackest sin. So, our triumph is complete.

I did not suppose that there could be any difference of opinion as to life's character. Probably there is none when we analyze it. It seems to me that our first duty is to recognize that life is tragedy and because this is so it gives us our opportunity. Until we admit the fact our capacity and responsibility are hidden. Tragedy is the raw material out of which victory and abiding splendor are woven. There can be no triumph without a war. The greater the war the more splendid the triumph. It is surely true that "man is born to trouble as the sparks fly upward." Tears and crying, pain and dying, hold a commanding place in mortality. But we conquer tears by weeping, pain by suffering, death by dying, *after a certain manner and with a certain motive.* This is the whole story of the great representative life, Jesus Christ. His precepts of course square with His practice.

The symbol of the Christian is the Cross which stands for concentrated pain, shame, sorrow, and death, out of which come freedom, glory, joy, and immortality. The true Christian faces life exactly as it is in its worst aspects fearlessly, joyously, triumphantly and reaches the summit of life's splendor by plunging into the stormiest stretches of mortality and garnering therein a freedom, an unquenchable exultation, a victory, an imperturbable peace and serenity which surpass anything else life has to offer. So St. Paul, speaking from his own experience, exclaims: "In all these things" (i.e., tribulation, distress, persecution, etc.), "we are supervictors (more than conquerors) through him that loves us." Our Lord's own words likewise declare life to be tragic: "In the world ye shall have tribulation: but be of good cheer; I have overcome the world."

Our chief danger is that we should try to escape suffering and trouble. It is bound to come, and if we have been using religion as an insurance against tribulation, when tribulation comes, the shock will be terrible. On the other hand, if we quietly accept the worst as being possible in our case, when it comes we deploy our spiritual forces so as to make the trouble, whatever it may be, an actual asset. This is being a supervictor. When evil strikes us we are never taken by surprise. We are not crushed, however much we suffer, and faith rises glorious in the night of gloom. Reckoning with life as a tragedy in which we must take our full share is the beginning of that human greatness that obscures all else that lays claim to greatness. It is this that makes men free and sunny and adventurers; they have nothing to fear in the worst because through the Cross and the present co-operation of the Victor (who is also the victim) of the Cross, the worst is an opportunity, clay wherewith to mold greatness, a whetstone on which to grind off our angles, a polishing wheel for our wit, our gladness, our buoyancy, a foil against which to display our immortality.

4. THE CITY THAT LIETH FOURSQUARE

If there is a touch of timelessness in man, there is also a touch of spacelessness. Consequently, when we try to get vision of the consummation of God's purposes, there must be eternity and infinity to satisfy us. It is only those who have become so engrossed in short views of life as, for the time being, to be blind to anything else, who do not find the need of some sense of God's mighty purpose as a daily support. Even with them there is that undercurrent of immortality which lends its aid when they are least conscious of it. The man who has the most tedious job can do it with zest if he is able to realize that it is an important part of a great scheme. On the other hand, those who are given large responsibilities can rise no higher than a mechanical fulfillment of them unless the inspiring force comes from what I have termed an out-of-door conception of life. The part must be in relation to the whole. Detach any undertaking, whether the manufacture of a piston-rod or the ordered completeness of any given organization, from the end for which it was set in operation, and it becomes valueless and unworthy of the attention of men. Apply this principle to the world and mankind and you will get a whole view of the human situation. Eschatology, which means the philosophy of finalities, is as essential to a rounded view of life as is the study of origins. Such study or any findings of physical science apart from a search for the ultimate purpose of God in creation, would be as meaningless and worthless as a piston-rod without an engine.

Doubtless most men, when they allow time for serious thinking, dimly believe that there is some far-off divine event toward which the whole creation moves. But unless it is pressed on their attention they do not easily apprehend that their effectiveness in their own local job, and their own inspiration in its performance, is in proportion to their clearness of vision of God's complete and ultimate plan. A visionless development of material resources and an enslavement of the secrets of the universe for our immediate enjoyment ends in "science without a soul." And if this war is being fought solely with a view to compass temporal ends, however lofty, it lacks sufficient motive and justification.

The least little scrap of humanity, the urchin of the streets, and the most influential and conspicuous leader of men, have alike the capacity and the right to know that there is a final goal and of what sort it is. The hymns of early childhood which open up limitless spaces and beauty to the child-mind are elements in giving the young the legitimate freedom. The constant pressing upon adult attention of the other world and the end of all things, not only has the sanction and example of Scripture, but also finds its justification in that craving for wholeness which is inherent in us. We must not be allowed to forget that here there is no continuing city. If we do, life is jolted out of perspective and the scale of values goes all awry.

This is a moment in which we should compel men to recognize that God has an ultimate and worthy purpose for mankind, and as far as may be, help them to see it. It is not a mere saving of the individual, though it includes that. It is something which can be expressed in terms of the nation, though the nation's fate, too, is included. Nor can the word democracy with its largest connotations satisfy the requirements of the case, though democracy also has its part to play in the whole. Even the establishment on earth of universal peace and righteousness is incomplete and provincial by the side of what God purposes and the instinct of the human soul expects and demands. It is something which, except in allegory, cannot find expression in terms of our planetary system, and the little conceit of time for which the sun is responsible. Eye hath not seen, nor ear heard, neither hath it entered into the heart of man, to perceive the good things which God has prepared for them that love Him.

The City that lieth foursquare is the home of an ordered society, big enough for redeemed mankind, for it is complete and whole with the completeness and holiness of God. The Kingdom of God, noble phrase! is the measure of the City.

This Kingdom is so humble and lowly that it can be and is within us. It is so comprehensive that it can contain mankind, and yet there is room. The capacity for sight is so great in one human soul that we can hold within ourselves the world that holds us. Perhaps this very fact is a testimony to the greatness of the Kingdom of God—certainly it bears witness to the fitness of that Kingdom for our make-up.

One of the just demands that the human heart urges is that the ultimate abode of men should be thoroughly human. By that I mean that every feature of the life shall respond to the expectation of every feature of our nature in its highest development. So the social aspect of Heaven is symbolized by the great multitude which no man could number. Men move up thither, with, as it would seem and as we would expect, the acuteness of self-consciousness worn down by a corporate consciousness which transcends our experience because of its vastness and its unity. The self-giving element rushes through the whole, vertically and horizontally, in full and pure stream. Racial and national characteristics and achievement are seen there, and lend special value to the whole. In other words, there is there all that which on earth we are trying to bring about in national life and in our scheme for a league of nations forming a commonwealth of mankind. Magnitude and order, according to Aristotle, make beauty. So that in Heaven there will be the satisfaction, according to the philosopher's definition, of a beauty which we yearn for, but which is out of reach because of the smallness of earth's population at any one time, even supposing we were able to secure order among those who were here.

Putting the completeness of the social life of Heaven over against the human normality of the Christ who had passed through death, and you have such a human society as would satisfy the idealism of ultra-Utopians. It is not unimportant to give emphasis to the fact that this society is human. Our life here with its temporal and temporary occupations and interests is not going to be magically changed into something quite different when death shall have waved his wand for the last time. The flow and continuity of human character is no more dislocated by death than it is by sleep. Everything worthy here, down to the playing of the boys and girls in the street, has its counterpart and full inwardness there. If I do not draw any sharp line of demarcation between Paradise and Heaven it is because Scripture does not encourage it or show me how. The suggestive value of Paradise is in its protection of the principle of growth or development which is so distinctively human. Whatever cataclysmic elements there are in life, they are a climax, a part of normal growth, and not a mere introduction of a foreign or interfering and explosive power. As Bergson has established, life is not cinematographic either in short or big jerks. It is a steady flow through mortality and death, and intermediacy and beyond. So when I speak of the society of Heaven I refer to the whole stretch of human life the other side of the grave.

That society is the major part of the human whole. It already exists. It is the greatest social reality there is, this City that lieth foursquare. Its white company is composed of all mankind since the first man, who have set their course thither and made it their deliberate and reiterated choice. In them history suddenly springs full-fledged into present life. It is no longer a tortuous procession winding through the vale of time, but a compact society, unified by a common motive, enjoying a fellowship of limitless extent and unmeasured richness. The

commonwealth of mankind is a fact that is the most towering
of all realities after God Himself. Not a passing pageant like
the nations of earth, it is permanent, for the City hath foundations builded of God. God has not stumbled in His purpose.
The eccentricities and limitations of time have not blocked
Him in His onward march with His children folded to His
breast. They are all there in unnumbered throng. Not one of
them is lost or misplaced.

As for our society on earth with its jangling discords and
frayed ends, it is to the great white company, a handbreadth
away, as a murky lowland stream to the clean ocean. Men
who have striven for well-ordered cities and states and a peaceful world, have there that for which they have striven. There
is no principle of order or culture or beauty or fellowship
which we hold precious on earth that is not in triumphant
operation in Heaven.

The wonderful thing is that this marvellous society is man's
handiwork in close co-operation with God's. We are building
it today as the men of yesterday built, each our share and
portion.

> For an ye heard a music, like enow
> They are building still, seeing the city is built
> To music, therefore never built at all,
> And therefore built for ever.

We must not take too seriously or too sadly the failures to
perfect our hopes and plans on earth, as long as our conviction
that God intends for us eventually to enter a complete life
abides unmarred, and our efforts toward that life persevere.
The Cross proclaims that we can, if we so choose, reign through
defeat, and that that for which we have striven makes its full
deposit only the other side of death. When we aim to make

ourselves and society whole, and set our lives upon our aim, failure is impossible. If we were to fail, God's throne would totter and the City that lieth foursquare dissolve. It is only the impatience of the mortal in us that lures us to despair and leads us out into the wilderness to die with inert hands, because the new sown grain refused to bear fruit in a night, and we expected one nation or one generation—or perhaps one little man!—to build the complete City in a day and to make Heaven unnecessary by converting earth into Heaven. Heaven must first live in the soul if the soul is to live in Heaven. Our chief responsibility on earth is not only to defend our vision of God and God's place from the blight of doubt, but also to commit ourselves to it more unreservedly today than yesterday. It is this that enables us to do the two things our high destiny requires of us. To contribute to the passing structure of mortal society something that will strengthen and invigorate, even if it does not perfect it. And to carry on in, rather than with, as a deposit of value for the City that lieth foursquare.

That City is so dependent upon us for a worthy contribution that without us it cannot lie quite foursquare. To go to the City without any trophy of our own winning would be humiliating. Even the lowliest and least endowed member of a family is ashamed to rejoice in the privileges built up by the activities of his parents and brethren without making some contribution of love, however tiny, to the common treasury. Only those well skilled in self-giving would be at home in a City where the sole competition is a vying with one another in the practice of love, and where the light which lightens the inhabitants is the Lamb Who laid down His life for mankind.

The society for which we are struggling, therefore, cannot

be realized in the nation, and not even in mankind, either today or tomorrow, any more than it was realized yesterday. For we are not creatures of time strutting across the tiny stage of space with imperial tread. We are the builders of the City that lieth foursquare. There is our ultimate goal, and all our schemes and efforts here must be directed toward it and, in all our motives and methods, be referred to it. The mankind of a day, even, is not a large enough unit in the terms of which to express our national character. When we talk of doing things for humanity's sake we mean for the whole race, reaching backwards and forwards and gathering up in its torrent the little present by means of which we make our offering.

Whether it be times of war or of peace our *modus operandi* must be such as will stand the test of life in the City that lieth foursquare. An *ad interim* religion for war time is as inconsistent as it would be for days of peace. To make terms with vice as a necessity of war is as abhorrent to an honest mind as any other compact with the devil. The one thing that gives war any place or justification in human affairs is that its soldiers are called to play their part with mind and body kept clean and ready for the pouring out of the soul into sacrificial death for a holy cause, and that all the forces of the nation, official and unofficial, are pledged to throw arms of protection and support about them.

We must not allow our contemplation of the complete order of the City that lieth foursquare to exclude our social whole on earth, for the link that binds the one to the other is organic, vital, and intimate. The "here" is the "there" in the process of becoming. All that vast multitude which composes the majority of the race from the beginning has been able to reach the goal only by the way we are now treading. When they

went to the City that lieth foursquare, they did not lose any
of the fragrance in which life on earth is rich, but carried it
with them. The tie that binds us together is the tie of a common
lot lived out with a common purpose, which purpose still
animates both those who are there and those who are here.
There memories of the past are quickened rather than dimmed
by timelessness, for all their "then" is in their "now." That
their vitality is shared with us, I am sure. The deposit they
left on earth is our chief asset. On it we build our own contribution. What direct efforts they are making for our edification and encouragement, to what extent an individual hand
there touches a life here, does not appear. But the self-giving
of the whole rushes earthward through generous arteries, and
gives us nourishment and cheer. We are compassed about with
a great cloud of witnesses—not idle observers but sympathetic
brethren.

There is a query today as to whether, except in mystical
fashion, there can be intercommunion between ourselves and
our friends yonder. Love chafes under the discipline of silence,
and seeks to break its bars. Psychic phenomena are being
called in to lend their aid and to produce voices of comfort.
They are studied and employed in the name of science, and
must be scientifically judged. They can be said to emanate
from the spirit world only by ignoring the more probable
hypothesis that they are the self-induced utterances of our own
desires, stored memories, and thought transference, evoked
from that subconscious life which is an established fact of
science. Until they are excluded from all possibility of finding
their explanation in this or any other cause, it is an unwar-
ranted conclusion to attribute them to disembodied spirits.
As phenomena opening up a new sphere for psychological

study they are interesting. As means of communicating with the world of spirits they are doubtful, perilous and unprofitable. He would indeed be rash who maintained that there are not degrees of nearness between the society of earth and that of the life beyond the grave, and that there has been no vocal or visible interchange of confidences between the two parts of the organic whole. But it is safe to say that such intercommunication is not the norm.

The veil that shuts out God and the deep things of God on earth from touch and sight and hearing is not lifted when men shed their material self, and climb to that fuller life of God which takes them from our conscious sphere. It is sufficient to know that the unlonely God has gathered them close to Him, and that in turning to Him we reach them, inevitably and securely. It is the mystical part of life that is the deepest. By means of it we apprehend Him, and through it He communicates with us. The logical presupposition, a presupposition supported by the experience of the ages, is that so far as those who are absent from the body can communicate with those of us who remain, it is normally through the same mystical faculty or element of our nature.

The last figure of Revelation is the first. Alpha is Omega, unchanged, unchangeable. He who is the source must be the goal of life. When all is said and done, when the words of the wise have exhausted themselves in trying to give suitable expression to the cravings and the capacity of human life, we turn to the inexhaustible wealth of God in whom alone is our sufficiency. He is all in all. His holiness is our wholeness.

The fullest vision of Him of which we are now capable is only an earnest of that which is to be. But in this we can rest secure that in future manifestations of Himself God will not surprise us by suddenly showing Himself to be something contrary to the basic revelation of His character. The groundwork of the Cross holds all the rest in its safe keeping. And all the comings of Jesus Christ in, and at the close of, time will be in loving self-giving even though they be in clouds and great glory. For His glorious Majesty, too, will bear the sign of the Cross.